M000098395

ONE AMERICA

ART GILLIAM

Published by Baldwin House Press, Memphis, TN
Copyright ©2014 Art Gilliam
All rights reserved.

Editor: Sally Wolfe | www.contentbysallywolfe.com

Cover and Interior design: Yvonne Parks | www.PearCreative.ca

Library of Congress Control Number: 2013913268

ISBN: 978-0-9897447-0-6 (softcover)
ISBN: 978-0-9897447-1-3 (hardcover)

ATTENTION CORPORATIONS, UNIVERSITIES, COLLEGES AND PROFESSIONAL ORGANIZATIONS: Quantity discounts are available on bulk purchases of this book for educational, gift purposes, or as premiums for increasing magazine subscriptions or renewals. Special books or book excerpts can also be created to fit specific needs. For information, please contact Baldwin House Press, 840 Bluebird Road; Memphis, TN 38116.

To those who joined the struggle to make America a better place

CONTENTS

Letting Go Of the Past

Nothing is more certainly written in the book of fate than that these people [slaves] are to be free. Nor is it less certain that the two races, equally free, cannot live in the same government. -Thomas Jefferson, Autobiography, 1821. ME 1:72

© Norbert Rehm/iStock/Thinkstock

INTRODUCTION

I was barely old enough to ride the bus alone. I was riding to Bethlehem Center, which was run by a few white Quakers who had come to the South to teach us arts and crafts. The center was in the neighborhood next to mine, but it was a long walk, so I was taking the bus. I was so proud that Mother was letting me ride the bus alone that day. She knew I wouldn't encounter any local white people, because the bus route began in our all-Negro neighborhood, and I didn't have to ride far enough to go through any white neighborhoods where they would begin boarding.

Sadly, and by design, Negroes, as we were called in the 1950s, had to ride the bus behind any white passengers who got on. That's what the sign said at the front of the bus. I remember that short bus ride in Memphis, my home town. It was a few years before Rosa Parks refused to sit in the back of a Montgomery, Alabama bus, triggering a bus boycott by Negroes, which was the initial incident that brought that boycott's leader, Martin Luther King, to the nation's attention. But that would all come later. At this time, I was only thinking about the arts and crafts awaiting me at Bethlehem Center and how proud I was that my mom trusted me to ride the bus alone. It meant I was a "big boy"!

If I had written a book proposal back then about what happened to that boy, it would have had the most improbable of story lines: he would leave the segregated South at thirteen to attend a nearly all-white New England prep school and seven years later would graduate from Yale University; he would earn a master's degree in actuarial science and go on to buy a radio station in Memphis; he would later marry a white girl living in Copenhagen, Denmark, and together from Memphis they would watch a fellow named Barack Hussein Obama, who had an African father and a white American mother, be sworn in as President of the United States.

Even the most liberal of book proposal reviewers would have relegated such a story to the fantasyland bin. That is, if the script and author made it past the nearest insane asylum, assuming the author was not lynched before having the opportunity to be committed. Yet here we are only a few decades later, and the story is in the category of nonfiction. I suppose it would be fair to say this could only happen in America. Yet on the way to this "only in America" ending are some very ugly stories that also happened in America. It is all part of life here and maybe everywhere really. We have our triumphs. We have our disillusionments. We have our challenges still to be met.

The story does not begin on that Memphis, Tennessee bus. It begins a little earlier, when I didn't even know I was a Negro. I was just a little boy with no awareness of race. Do you remember a time when you had no awareness of race? What an uncomplicated world! At some point life changes all of that. For now though, let's go back to that age of innocence where there was no race, to a place where for me life was happy and simple—in Mama's kitchen begging for a johnnycake.

THE AGE OF INNOCENCE

CHAPTER ONE
CHILDHOOD IN THE SOUTH

My dad was driving to work daydreaming, as people so often do when they are driving on a lazy day. A looming traffic jam brought back his attention. To avoid the traffic backup, he slowly veered his car into another lane, but that lane wasn't moving much either. A white policeman, who was trying to direct the traffic, walked up to the car window and belligerently told him to back the car out of the lane. But another car had followed my dad into the lane, and he could not move his car. The policeman continued to loudly insist that he move the car. Dad told the policeman he was stuck between cars and could not move. The cop continued to angrily raise his voice. Dad then asked the cop to move the car for him.

The cop apparently decided that dad was one of those uppity niggers of the 1940s and drew his revolver. Realizing he was in danger, dad quickly threw himself across the front seat as the cop fired the gun. The bullet slammed into the passenger door on the inside of the car. If my mom had been in the car that day or if my dad had not been athletic enough to drop back across the seat in time for the bullet to miss him, you would not be reading this, because I had not yet been born.

Dad told me this story when I was very young, maybe five. Looking back on it, I think he told me the story so I would understand that white cops in the South, who were the only cops in the South in those brutally segregated years, were very dangerous.

All in all though, we did not talk much in my family about white racism when I was very young. Negro parents deferred that conversation until later so their children could, at least for a brief period, enjoy a happy childhood without having to deal with the burden of being regarded as second class citizens.

Mom and Dad had to deal with the exclusions and problems, and sometimes even the horrors, of being Negroes virtually every day of their lives. Despite the frustrations and disappointments they faced, they sheltered me from most of those things so that I could remain happy as a child. And my childhood was especially happy on those Saturdays when Mama cooked johnnycakes.

"Mama, can I have the johnnycake ... pleeease?" I asked my grandmother.

I always called her "Mama," and my mother, who was her daughter, was "Mother." Every Saturday morning, Mama would make homemade biscuits. It was 1950, when homemade biscuits were really home made. Mama would make the dough from scratch, and she had a little round metal cylinder, about an inch high, that she used for cutting the biscuits one by one out of the flattened dough. As she pressed the cylinder down on the dough on the cutting board, each cut would form a rounded disc. When she had cut all the biscuits she could make out of the flattened dough, there were several small pieces left over. Mama would gather up all those small pieces in her hand and knead them together into one big irregular biscuit. It didn't have the neat powder puff shape of the other biscuits and was about three times the size. Mama called it the johnnycake, and it just seemed to taste better than the other ones.

That was our Saturday morning ritual. Mama cooked biscuits. I begged for the johnnycake. It always ended with me being awarded the prize, but only after a little teasing.

"Leola (that was Mother), don't you want this johnnycake?" she would ask.

"Let me think about it," Mother would answer.

"No, no!" I would insist at the top of my voice. "I want the johnnycake!"

"You know, I'll bet Herman (that was Daddy) is going to want this johnnycake when he comes to breakfast," Mama would add.

"Don't give it to Daddy! Give it to meee! Give it to meee!" And when the teasing was over, Mama always gave me the johnnycake. What a delight!

That was my world at the time. There was Daddy, Mother, Mama, Falla, and me. Falla was our black Scottish terrier who was there with me from the time I was born until the day he died of old age years later. I was an only child, so Falla was my playmate. In 1950, life for me was pretty much happy and carefree. When I look at our pictures taken then, I see an innocent little boy with bright eyes and a happy smile. I think most children in America begin life in a similar way. Their race doesn't make any difference, or their religion, or social status, or the like. There is simply a wonderful innocence where we love everyone around us, if they will allow us to. We begin life in this age of innocence.

I didn't know I was considered a second class citizen in the South. I didn't know I wouldn't be allowed to go to the zoo or the movies except on certain days, or that there were such things as separate drinking fountains designated for "colored" people. I didn't know I was supposed to ride in the back of the bus. One day Mother would have to explain all of these things to me. What a heavy heart a mother must have when she has to explain to her "baby" that he is not like everyone else and that somehow the fact that he is a Negro makes him, in the eyes of some, less worthy.

I didn't know about any of this in 1950. I was just a happy little boy who wanted that johnnycake, and Mama always gave it to me. I was her only grandchild, so she spoiled me at times. But she was kind to people in general. Not a tall woman, she was probably about average height for that era, neither heavy nor skinny but maybe slightly stocky. What I most remember though is that she was always nice, except for one time that she became absolutely livid.

She had taken me to the fairgrounds. It was colored day. All the vendors were the same ones that were there when whites went to the fair, which is to say that all of the vendors were white even on colored day at the fairgrounds. Mama bought me a soft ice cream that they swirl out of the machine. Mama turned away, and the lady licked my ice cream just before she handed it to me. I started crying and told Mama. She went off, and that may be an understatement. The lady insisted that she did not lick the ice cream; however Mama told her in no uncertain terms to give me another one.

At the time, I did not fully appreciate the gravity of this situation. Here was Mama, who had been born only about thirty years after slavery ended, trying to make this white woman vendor on the one colored day at the fair give me another ice cream. The lady kept insisting she had not licked the ice cream, but with a very mean look she finally relented and gave me another one. As we left the vendor's booth, Mama was mumbling that white people thought they could do anything and get away with it. It is the only time I saw Mama really angry.

As much racial injustice as there was in that era, we did not dwell on it in our household. From my point of view as a young child, we were simply a happy family where the opportunity for a practical joke was seldom passed by, like the one they pulled on me one April first.

The doorbell rang. I was just waking up, and it was time to dress for school. I heard Mother downstairs talking to someone at the front door.

"Oh, come on in, Miss Sanders," she said. Miss Sanders was my sixth grade teacher. "Yes, Art's here. He's about to get dressed for school."

Mom then hurried up the stairs.

"Art, get dressed," she said. "Miss Sanders is here, and she's not going to be able to go to school today."

I wasn't fully awake and looked at her a little befuddled.

"Miss Sanders wants someone to take over the class today and she thinks you'd be just the right person, so she's here to talk to you about it."

Suddenly, I was wide awake.

"Me?" I asked, beaming with much more than just a little pride.

"Yes. Clean up and get dressed, and put on your best clothes. It's an important job!"

I don't think I had ever gotten dressed quite that fast. I then hurried to the top of the stairs, and Mother gave me a nod signaling that I looked just fine for the task ahead. Dad looked on approvingly as well.

"Go on downstairs. Miss Sanders is waiting for you!" Mom said.

I rushed to the bottom of the stairs and looked all around the living room. Miss Sanders was nowhere in sight. Then I heard raucous laughter coming from the top of the stairs.

"April fool!" Mom and Dad laughed in unison. Mom had rung the doorbell herself and carried on a mock conversation with Miss Sanders. I was the April fool.

I walked slowly back up the stairs, head down, like a dog with its tail between its legs. Mom and Dad were laughing almost uncontrollably. I finally had to admit that it was pretty funny, and we ended up having a good laugh together.

That's the way it was for me growing up. It was lighthearted. It was fun. I was insulated from the problems of the world. My mom and dad kept it that way even as they were dealing every day with the difficulties and exclusions of being Negroes in America, especially in the South. I look back now in deep admiration for the way they kept life at home so happy and carefree in the midst of the struggles they were facing because of race. They wanted my life to be a happy one. In the final analysis though, the only way I happened to be there at all was because of a bullet that missed.

Art Gilliam as a young boy in Memphis

CHAPTER TWO
JACKIE ROBINSON AND THE BROOKLYN DODGERS

As I grew older but was still in my childhood, there was relatively little exposure to the segregation and discrimination that pervaded society in the South. Even as late as our pre-teen years, my playmates and I lived largely separated from the white world. We lived in a Negro America. It was a happy place for kids, probably because we were not involved in the day-to-day interaction with whites that was inevitable for adults but not necessary for children.

Virtually everyone in my world at that time was Negro. We went to separate schools. We had our own restaurants, our own theaters, our own churches. We even had our own funeral homes. The fact that these were the ONLY schools, ONLY restaurants, ONLY theaters, ONLY churches, and ONLY funeral homes for us was not something we considered as children. We were happy kids living in our own segregated world. It was a society within a society. Literally, if you didn't live past your early teen years, you might never have known that you were considered by the broader society to be a lower form of humanity. You would have been born in a Negro hospital, raised in a Negro South, and buried by a Negro funeral home after your funeral at a Negro church.

The church was the mainstay of our community. It is ironic that as a society we worshipped Jesus in separate churches, Negro and white. Today, more than fifty years later, this is still largely the same. The only real difference is that today we refer to ourselves as black, so the separate churches are black and white instead of Negro and white.

Mother was determined to make sure I went with her to church every Sunday, whether Daddy went or not. She always made me sit still and quietly listen to the sermon. She loved to go to church, and of course, she wanted to make sure that her son got a proper indoctrination in the Spirit. Praise God that the minister was actually pretty good, because church was not the place where I wanted to be at that age. Reverend Blair Hunt preached good sermons. He took parables from the Bible and wove them into meaningful stories about life. At the appropriate time, I would even say a little "Amen!" along with the rest of the congregation. But I was so glad when he finished that I would whisper "Hallelujah!" under my breath and look up and smile at Mother, who nodded approvingly. Hallelujah, it was time to go to the corner store near the church for ice cream!

Many years later in life, after I had completed college and was not spending much time in church, Mother was surprised at how well versed I was on stories from the Bible. I felt I had to let her know the reason was that I recalled many of those sermons she made me sit through every single Sunday when I was a little boy. In retrospect, it was a good thing.

Sundays after church, in the spring and summer, Daddy would take me to see the Memphis Red Sox play baseball at Martin Stadium. The stadium was near downtown Memphis, and the team and the stadium were principally owned by two Negro doctors, brothers W. S. and J. B. Martin. It was our Negro League team that played the teams from other cities—Kansas City, Birmingham, Chicago, New York, and others. We went to Martin Stadium regularly to see them play, and the Red Sox players were heroes to me.

One day Daddy said that instead of going to see the Red Sox the coming Sunday, we were going to drive to St. Louis for the weekend to see a "major league" baseball game. The only major league I knew anything about was the league the Red Sox played in, so I wasn't sure why we would go to St. Louis when we could just stay home and go see the Red Sox. Nonetheless, I was very happy about the upcoming trip. I had never been very far from home except to the country, which is what we called the farmland and rural areas that stretched for miles around Memphis. St. Louis at the time seemed to me like some mystical place far away. In actuality, it was only about three hundred miles from Memphis.

The trip was much more profound for Daddy than it was for me at the time. He wasn't just taking me to St. Louis to see a major league baseball game. He was taking me to see the St. Louis Cardinals play the Brooklyn Dodgers. More specifically, Daddy was taking me to St. Louis to see Jackie Robinson play baseball.

"Daddy," I asked. "Who's Jackie Robinson?"

"He's the first Negro to ever play baseball in the major leagues," he replied.

"But the Memphis Red Sox are Negroes, aren't they?" I continued.

"That's not quite the same as the major leagues," he said. I kind of understood but not really. I still wasn't quite sure why we drove all the way to St. Louis to see a baseball game. What I was sure of was that it was a great trip, and I was having a good time.

When I was a little older and better understood the importance of Jackie Robinson, I became, along with most Negroes, deeply loyal fans of the Brooklyn Dodgers. There were tears of joy in our eyes when Jackie and the Dodgers, who had a number of Negro players by that time, finally beat the New York Yankees in the 1955 World Series. But on that day when we went to St Louis, I was just a bright-eyed little kid who didn't fully appreciate exactly why we went. I did figure that this Jackie Robinson must have been a heck of a fellow if we went all that way to see him play baseball. What Daddy knew then, and what I came to realize some years later, was that I would forever remember the significance of that day when my dad took me to St. Louis to see Jackie Robinson play baseball at Sportsman's Park.

THE AWAKENING

CHAPTER THREE
THE BACK OF THE BUS

I assumed, in the way children assume, that we would all live happily ever after in the world as I knew it and believed it to be. It was inevitable that this bubble of innocence would burst. Negroes lived in a shadow society wherein we tried to emulate the white society by whom we were subjugated. The happy world I had come to know at a young age was an illusion. One day the illusionist would wave his wand, and with a puff of smoke my fantasy world would be gone forever and the real world would appear on life's stage.

The first glimpse I had of the reality of segregation happened on a Memphis bus, which Mother and I boarded at the stop down the street from our house. I don't recall where we were going or when it was, but I was very young, maybe six or seven years old. What I do remember is that while Mother was paying the driver the fare, I turned and sat down on the first available seat. No one else was on the bus. We were the first to board, because we lived near the first stop the bus made on its route to downtown. When Mother paid the fare and turned and saw where I was sitting, she said, "We're not going to sit there."

Like so many questioning youngsters I asked, rather loudly, "Why not?" I won't forget the look she gave me. It was one of those looks only a mother can give you and that lets you know she is serious, and it is time for you to shut up. There was, though, another aspect to the way she looked at me that went beyond just being upset. She was embarrassed. I had caught her by surprise.

She simply said, "We are going to sit farther back." Her tone told me to just follow her, and that day I didn't ask any more questions. I did not know at the time the significance of the sign painted clearly on the front of the bus above the driver: "Colored passengers occupy rear seats first." As I grew older, I developed a very deep resentment over that message on all the Memphis buses. It is something I can never forget. It was my first encounter with the myriad signs throughout Memphis and the rest of the segregated South that stamped a badge of inferiority on all the Negroes who lived there.

Negro mothers must have contemplated painfully for long hours about what they would tell their children as they began to grow into an awareness of segregation, discrimination, and exclusion. How do you explain this to a child without breaking the child's heart and spirit? Part of the answer depends on what the mother has told herself and how she has rationalized her status in society and assimilated it into her own psyche. My mom simply told me

I was as good as anyone else but that we nonetheless would be sitting in the back of the bus.

The signs reflecting the segregation in the South were everywhere. They read *Colored* and *White*. If it was public drinking water, there were two fountains, one for each race. If it was a theater that even allowed us to be there at all, there were two clearly marked entrances. The *White* entrance was the usual front entrance. The *Colored* entrance was typically around the corner and led upstairs to the upper balcony seats. In the railroad and bus stations, there was the *Colored Waiting Room* and the *White Waiting Room*. At the largest department store in Memphis, there were four restrooms side by side: *White Men*; *White Women*; *Colored Men*; *Colored Women.*

They were separate and anything but equal. The store didn't tell us our money was not welcomed there. It told us to feel free to spend our money and while we were there to be treated like the inferior citizens they believed us to be. The supreme irony in the South was at the courthouses, where "Justice is blind." Throughout the courthouse were those same white and colored signs. Indeed, justice was blind. It was blind to the rights of colored people.

As I grew into a young teenager, I often rode the bus alone. I never sat in the back, but since I lived in a Negro neighborhood, it didn't matter from a racial standpoint because most of my bus travels were within the neighborhood where only two or three white people would ever be riding anyway. I will always remember this one occasion when I was going out of the neighborhood to downtown. If you rode the bus downtown, then you would pass through white neighborhoods where more white passengers would get on board.

I was riding on about the fourth seat from the front and not paying much attention to anything that was happening on the bus. I was more or less daydreaming when I suddenly snapped out of the daydream and became aware that there were several people who were standing. Yet there were plenty of seats available. I then realized that all of the people who were standing were white people and that all the seats in front of me had been filled by other white people. The available seats on the bus were all behind me, and the white people on the bus were standing, because they refused to sit behind me. They were staring at me.

I was too proud to move back, but I was nervous. I tried not to show it, and I just looked away out the window hoping my stop would come soon so I could get off. But before we got to my stop, the bus stopped and did not move again for quite a while. I just kept looking out the window. What had happened was that the white bus driver had summoned a white policeman to move me to the back so the white passengers could sit down. The policeman, gun holstered (and I was very aware of the fact that he had a gun), approached me and demanded that I move back. I was truly nervous. I knew I was not going to move back, but I also knew I could not win a fight with an armed policeman. I got up and walked to the front of the bus. When I got there, I got off at the front exit and walked the remaining mile to my destination.

From our point of view as a race of people, the police, all of whom were white, embodied all the white hatred and oppression that existed in the South. That's why colored people, and then Negroes, and then blacks always hated, or at best mistrusted, the police. The police were the instruments for enforcement of the evils of the society.

Drinking fountain on the County Courthouse lawn. Halifax, North Carolina

Library of Congress, Prints & Photographs Division, FSA/OWI Collection, [LC-DIG-fsa-8a03228]

Rest stop for Greyhound bus passengers on the way from Louisville, Kentucky to Nashville, Tennessee, with separate accommodations for colored passengers.

Library of Congress, Prints & Photographs Division, FSA/OWI Collection, [LC-USW3-037919-E]

CHAPTER 4
BROWN V. TOPEKA

To separate [Negro children] from others of similar age and qualifications solely because of their race generates a feeling of inferiority as to their status in the community that may affect their hearts and minds in a way unlikely ever to be undone . . .We conclude that in the field of public education the doctrine of 'separate but equal' has no place. Separate educational facilities are inherently unequal.

Brown v. Board of Education of Topeka, 347 U.S. 438 [1954]

I was only eleven years old in 1954 when the Supreme Court of the United States rendered its decision in the case of Brown v. Board of Education of Topeka. The circumstances of the case were straightforward. In 1951, a Negro railroad worker named Oliver Brown had sued the Topeka, Kansas Board of Education for not permitting his daughter, Linda Brown, to attend Sumner Elementary School. Sumner was an all-white school near her home. Brown's legal argument was presented by Thurgood Marshall, who was the chief counsel for the National Association for the Advancement of Colored People (NAACP) and later became the first Negro justice to sit on the United States Supreme Court.

The court unanimously ruled that requiring Linda to go to a Negro school farther away from her home constituted racial segregation in public schools, which the court found to be unconstitutional. The justices ruled that segregated schools deprive minorities of equal educational opportunities, and they further found that segregation reinforces the concept that Negroes are inferior to whites. The singular phrase that stood out in my mind, and which has remained vivid for me throughout my life, was the declaration that separate but equal is inherently unequal.

The court declared that separation violates the Fourteenth Amendment to the Constitution, which provides that all American citizens have the right to equal protection under the law. This ruling in Brown v. Topeka overturned an 1896 case, Plessy v. Ferguson, which established the "separate but equal" doctrine that had been the underlying basis for widespread segregation throughout the South for more than fifty years. It was due to the Plessy v. Ferguson ruling that racial segregation with its system of inferior facilities for Negroes was perpetuated by law.

I have a vivid recollection of the joy my mom and dad felt when the Brown v. Topeka ruling was handed down. It was like a Day of Jubilee. As they interpreted it at the time, it was a vindication of Negroes as first class citizens in this country. My dad found special significance in the fact that the decision was unanimous. With all nine justices being in agreement, the ruling was understood by many of us to mean that Negroes were now American citizens equal to whites and with the same rights as whites. That assessment, in retrospect, may have rested more on hopes and aspirations than on the reality of what would actually happen.

Our jubilation was premature. The case was not the end of the quest for justice and equality but only one important step forward in what would prove to be a long, arduous, and bitter struggle. Civil rights changes in America did not come by leaps and bounds but by incremental steps. In many ways, it was progress by a successive process of two steps forward and one step backward. The promise of equal protection under the law was a step forward that would soon give way to disillusionment. The tragedies that would follow were anything but affirmation of equal protection. One tragedy in particular was so heinous that it would resonate indelibly for a lifetime in many of our hearts and minds.

CHAPTER FIVE
THE MURDER OF EMMETT TILL

The name Emmett Till had not consciously come to my mind for many years, and yet as I was outlining this book, it kept coming increasingly into my thoughts. There was something ominously compelling about it. I knew I had to resurrect it and research it, and as I did so, I realized that what it represented to me had been repressed for a very long time. When my memory of his murder fully resurfaced, I would lay awake at night struggling with the images and with the fear they engendered. I had to come to terms with the fact that more than fifty years later, I had not fully reconciled the effect on my very young mind of what had happened to Emmett Till in Money, Mississippi in 1955. I was only twelve years old. He was fourteen. I did not know him, but what was done to him profoundly impacted me.

It happened during that summer. Ironically, it was only a little more than a year after the Supreme Court had ruled that all our citizens are entitled to equal protection under the law. Emmett Till lived in Chicago, Illinois and was visiting relatives in northwest Mississippi in a little Mississippi River Delta town called Money. His "crime" was that he reportedly whistled at a white woman, Carolyn Bryant, at Bryant's Grocery and Meat Market, where he and some other Negro boys had gone to buy candy and soft drinks. The store was owned by Carolyn Bryant and her husband Roy.

It was after this alleged incident that Roy Bryant and his half brother, J. W. Milam, were among a group who abducted Emmett Till from his uncle's home on the night of August 28 and murdered him. He was brutally beaten by his white captors. One of his eyes was gouged out before he was shot in the head and thrown into the Tallahatchie River. A seventy pound cotton gin fan was tied around his neck with barbed wire. It was three days after the murder that two boys who were fishing discovered and retrieved the body.

At the trial of Bryant and Milam, the all-white, all-male jury deliberated only sixty-seven minutes before acquitting them both. One juror with a frighteningly cavalier attitude said, "If we hadn't stopped to drink pop, it wouldn't have taken us too long." [1] Such was the regard for the life of a Negro child in the Mississippi Delta of the 1950s. The full story became known when Bryant and Milam, safe from further charges due to double jeopardy, admitted in a story written by William Bradford Huie in *Look* magazine that they had indeed killed Emmett Till. Their confession, coupled

---

1   Emmett Till, Wikipedia.org

with a decision made by Till's mother, gave fresh momentum to the civil rights movement.

Mamie Till Bradley, Emmett's mother, insisted that the body be returned to Chicago for burial. The corpse was so disfigured that it could not be identified except by a ring that Emmett Till wore that was his father's. Despite efforts to dissuade her, his mother insisted that the coffin be left open. The grotesque appearance of the body was difficult to view. I saw the picture of it, as did many throughout the world, in a photograph printed in *Jet* magazine. In Chicago, a Negro newspaper, *The Chicago Defender*, reported: "All [who saw the body] were shocked, some horrified and appalled. Many prayed, scores fainted and practically all, men, women, and children wept."[2]

An article in the *Daily Worker* also recounted the horror: "Strong young men were weeping openly without shame; some were shaken with uncontrollable cries of grief; others fainted as they saw the mute evidence of the unspeakable barbarity of the white supremacist lynchers."[3]

Mamie Till Bradley was quoted in several papers as saying that she wanted all the world "to see what they did to my boy."

The picture of the body and the story of how and why he died were overwhelming for me at that time. While leaving the casket open surely had a significant impact on the civil rights movement, it further magnified the already horrendous effect of the incident on

2   *Chicago Defender*, September 10, 1955

3   Carl Hirsch, *Daily Worker*, September 10, 1955

a twelve-year-old Negro boy growing up only ten miles from the Mississippi state line.

Emmett Till as a young boy
© Dr. Ernest C. Withers, Sr. courtesy of the WITHERS FAMILY TRUST
www.witherscollection.org

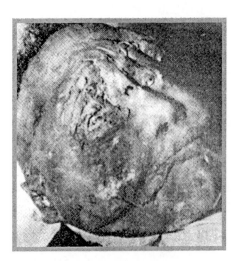

Emmett Till, mutilated and murdered
© Dr. Ernest C. Withers, Sr. courtesy of the WITHERS FAMILY TRUST
www.witherscollection.org

CHAPTER SIX
LEAVING THE SOUTH

Mother was a very strong woman. I only saw her cry twice. The first time was when she watched from the outdoor boarding area as Daddy and I were leaving on an airplane bound for Connecticut. It was 1956, and he was taking me to the prep school I would be attending in the small Connecticut township of Simsbury. I could see her wiping tears from her eyes under her sunglasses. She knew she would never again be an everyday mom to me, her only child, except maybe during the summers. That made her sad. Yet she accepted it, because she realized that by leaving the South, I would have a chance at a better education and a better future. The murder of Emmett Till in the summer of 1955 doubtless played a role in my parents' decision. Not only did the North offer better opportunity, but the vicious killing of Emmett Till demonstrated that the lives of innocent Negro children in the South were at risk to the racist elements that permeated the landscape.

My mom and dad weighed the difficulty I might have at such a young age adjusting to an alien environment versus the psychological impact of remaining in a racist environment that would certainly reinforce the idea that I was a second class citizen. They decided that despite the risk that I might not be able to make the emotional adjustment, they would send me out of the South.

The school year 1955-1956 thereby became my last year with the friends and classmates I loved so dearly at Hamilton High School. I completed the tenth grade, the youngest in my class. I had entered the tenth grade at the age of twelve, and I was "ahead of myself," as they called it in those days. At that time the schools in Memphis tested students periodically and placed them in the grade indicated by the testing, rather than the grade that corresponded to their chronological age. My mom had spent countless hours tutoring me. As a result, when I was tested in Memphis the first time, I was placed in the fourth grade at the age of six, and I had remained ahead of myself from that point forward.

All of my classmates were at least three years older than I was, so I was not as strong and physically developed as the other boys. Several of them became like big brothers and looked out for me, especially when there was a fight. And fighting was kind of a way of life in those days, particularly at lunch time on the playground. The various divisions of the grade would often fight each other for supremacy. On any given day in the tenth grade, for example, grade 10A might have a free-for-all with grade 10B. Whenever the fight started, it seemed like every day at least one kid in one of the other divisions would start the lunch time fight yelling, "I've got the little guy!"

Unfortunately for me, I was the little guy. But several of my classmates—Millard, Black, Edward Earl, and Louis—would make sure no one hurt me really badly. I think they just felt sorry for me, because I was so young and so small. I eventually became bigger than most of them. I grew to be over six feet and more than two hundred pounds, but in those days I was just a little shrimp.

When I went away to Westminster School in Connecticut, I left all my classmates and friends behind. I was literally exchanging my life as a Negro child from an all-Negro environment in the racist South for a new life in an overwhelmingly white environment. It is central to my life that my mom and dad decided that in order for me to have a better life, I would need to leave the South. They were basically turning my development into adulthood over to strangers who would guide me in an environment where I was not automatically perceived as inferior and who would, by and large, try to ensure that I had an equal right to "life, liberty, and the pursuit of happiness." It was something mom and dad could not provide for me in Memphis in the 1950s.

They had both grown up in the South. Dad was from a little town in rural South Carolina called Newberry. Both his mother and father died before he entered high school, and he lived for a time with his dad's sister Sarah and her family in Newberry. A couple of years later he moved to New York City where some of his other aunts and uncles had moved. He remained in New York and never finished high school. Yet he often talked to me about how important education was. He was really the driving force behind my going to prep school in Connecticut. He is also the reason I went to Yale. I think he read somewhere that it was the best college in America, and that must have shaped his vision.

Dad played professional baseball for three years for the New York team in the Negro Leagues. He left baseball for the more lucrative job of being a Pullman porter on the railroad, a top-of-the-line job for Negroes in those days. One of his fellow porters, Porterfield Caruthers, would eventually become his father-in-law. He married Porterfield's daughter, Leola, who became my mother. They named me Herman Arthur Gilliam, Jr. after my dad. They were married for more than thirty years before he passed away.

Mother was more serious, and even somber, at times, but Daddy had a great sense of humor, and she laughed easily with him. By Negro standards at that time, she had an extraordinary education. She finished college at all-Negro Tennessee State University in Nashville, her hometown. She then went to graduate school at Columbia University in New York where she received her master's degree in English. She moved back to Nashville after graduate school, and she and my dad settled there. She became a school teacher, and he became an insurance agent at Negro-owned Universal Life Insurance Company which operated in several southern states. While he had the vision to see a special path for my education, she took care of all the arduous training that really made it possible. She tutored me from as far back as I can remember, and she was so good at it that I tested at the fourth grade level when I was only six years old.

I never thought of my parents as being exceptional when I was growing up. They were just Mother and Daddy to me, and they never touted themselves. They spent more energy uplifting others. Looking back on it though, they were well ahead of their time. He steadily rose through the ranks at Universal from an agent to vice-president in charge of all agency operations. As a result, we moved to Memphis where the company's headquarters were located, and that is where I grew up. It was the success they had, even in the segregated and deeply discriminatory South in which we lived, that gave them the opportunity to consider sending me over one thousand miles from home to New England. They knew they would not be able to visit me often and that I would seldom be able to return except for a couple of holidays each year and the summers. They knew it would be a tremendous culture shock going from an all-Negro environment to an essentially all-white environment. They knew they were placing me in a situation that could make me or possibly break me. They prayed that it would all work out. It would be years after they made that heart wrenching decision before they would really know whether they had done the right thing. In parenting it just comes with the territory that you make the best decisions you can at the time; it is often years before you really know if it worked out for the better. It is especially difficult for a caring mother to send her only child so far away from home at such an early age. In later years Mother came to know that she and Daddy were doing the right thing that day in 1956 when she cried at the airport as Daddy and I were leaving for Connecticut. The only other time I ever saw her cry was on July 28, 1973. Daddy had a heart attack wading in the ocean off the beach at Montego Bay, Jamaica. That was the day he died.

CHAPTER SEVEN
"COON, BABY!"

The choice of Westminster School in Simsbury, Connecticut, which is only a few miles from Hartford, was a lucky one for me. It was a very warm, nurturing environment, and I needed it. I was the only Negro in my class of forty students, all boys. It was quite a change. From an academic standpoint, I had been virtually a straight A student in my tenth grade year at Hamilton, but I did the tenth grade (or Fourth Form, as they call it in prep school) again at Westminster. Most of the courses were ones I had not studied before. And the few I had studied were on a far more advanced level than had been offered at Hamilton.

From a social and emotional standpoint, I faced a huge adjustment. I felt uprooted and in many ways isolated and uncertain, going from an all-Negro environment in the South to this new white environment in the North. I could tell endless stories about what it was like, but I will share this one. I had heard it said that all Negroes looked alike (to white people). I knew though unequivocally that each Negro had his or her own individual characteristics. What I found to be the truth was that in fact it was white people who looked alike. Of course, I could distinguish a dark-haired Italian from a blonde Swede, but when I first went to Westminster, that was about the limit of my ability to discern. I had never seen so many white people in one place at one time, and to my consternation, they practically all looked alike to me!

Over time of course I realized that just as every Negro has his or her own individual personality and characteristics, so does every white person. That may have been one of the greatest lessons I eventually learned in my new environment—that even though we have our individual differences, people are basically the same in terms of what we want in life and what we deserve from life. It only takes getting to know people to recognize how alike we really are. In coming to understand that, I came also to recognize that the only real differences between my new classmates at Westminster and my former classmates at Hamilton were differences in opportunity and self-esteem.

When I was home during the summers, I began to realize I was growing apart from some of my old friends in many ways. My accent was gone. I didn't understand the new slang terms. Yet there was a bond between us that was not to be broken. It grew from our common experiences over many years at Hamilton. And no matter what distance came between us or how different our social and cultural experiences were, there was always a part of me that was this little Negro boy growing up in an all-Negro school in Memphis.

Sometimes my former classmates asked me what white people were like in the North. I told them that many white people treated me very well. It was not like the South. There was no "back of the bus," there were no *colored* and *white* drinking fountains. The palpable racial hatred that existed in the South, especially in Mississippi and parts of the Deep South, was absent. Yet there were prejudiced white people in the North as well. One particular incident taught me a lesson I would carry with me forever. The background to the story is that I did not know anything about Jews when I entered prep school. I did not even know Judaism was a religion. I had never heard of the Holocaust and that Jews had been subjected to genocide. I was not familiar with any stereotypes of Jews. In my world in the South, Jews were just never mentioned by any Negroes I had ever been around.

One day one of the white kids on my dorm floor at Westminster told a joke about another kid, Friedman, who was not on the floor at the time. Friedman had broken his arm and was wearing a cast. The "joke" was what Friedman allegedly said when he broke his arm: "This is going to cost me plenty of money to fix." It was told with what I later realized was a mock New York Jewish accent. Well, I laughed with the others. I thought it was funny, in and of itself, that anyone who had broken their arm would be more concerned about the cost of repairing the arm than the seriousness of the injury. I was not aware of any stereotype about Jews being cheap, nor did I even know Friedman was Jewish. So at the halftime of our next basketball game, I told this joke to my teammates exactly the way it had been told to me.

It was met with silence, and one of my teammates leaned over and whispered to me, "Do you know Federbush (another teammate) is Jewish?" It took a short while for it to sink in that I had just told a racist joke about Jews, but somehow I did get it. I was not just embarrassed that I had told the joke. I was almost equally embarrassed that I had not been aware that the joke was an affront to Jews. I wanted to tell Federbush the whole story, but I wasn't sure how to say how stupid I was and how sorry I was in the same conversation. I couldn't believe I had been that dumb, let alone that I was about to try to convince him that I was that naïve. I decided to simply say "I'm sorry."

He was more gracious and forgiving of me than I was of myself. As I went on in life, I came to discover that Jews would be disproportionately among the most liberal and generous people I would ever meet. The lesson I learned that day at halftime was one I would carry with me the rest of my life—never again. Never again I would I spend any time with prejudiced people. It can rub off and tarnish you. Or as my grandmother used to say, "If you lay down with dogs, you'll wake up with fleas."

It didn't take long to figure out that the same group of white kids who were prejudiced against Jews were also prejudiced against me and other Negroes. One day I was on the baseball practice field with some of them, and we were doing team drills. The coach repeatedly hit the ball to the outfield and the outfielders threw it back to home plate. Each time an outfielder got the ball and threw it, we all yelled, "Home, baby! Home, baby! Home, baby!" It was part of having a spirited practice. For a small group of the players, "Home, baby!" evolved into "Hoome (as in doom), baby! Hoome, baby! Hoome, baby!" And then it became "Coon, baby! Coon, baby! Coon, baby!" I pretended it as if I had not heard it.

The coach went over to one of them and put an end to it. It was the same clique that had been involved in the Jewish joke.

A few months later when we were all graduating, the more prejudiced kids had not been accepted in the preferred colleges, if they had been accepted in any college at all. In later years after graduation, those same kids were not very supportive of Westminster, nor did they come to the class reunions. They generally were not getting along as well in life as the kids who did not harbor prejudices. Prejudice, whether whites against blacks or vice versa, has a way of sorting itself out over time so that the bad guys usually lose and the good guys usually win.

The classmates I was closest to were more open in their views, and they were largely going to Yale, Harvard, Princeton, and the other Ivy League schools. I had been accepted at Yale. I must admit I did take some satisfaction in knowing that the kids who were yelling "Coon, baby!" weren't achieving their academic aspirations, while I was on my way to fulfilling my dad's dream that I would one day attend Yale University.

My sense of accomplishment soon gave way to a disturbing reality. I had gone to Yale, but many of my schoolmates from Hamilton, some of whom I knew were brilliant, had gone to jail. That was sad for me, because by that time I had begun to recognize how the systematic assault on the self-esteem of Negroes in the South impacted our psyche and our ability to achieve in life. Not all of my classmates at Hamilton became "lost," but many of them did. I knew deep in my heart that they never deserved the hardships and disillusionment that life had visited upon them. When I returned home that summer, I recognized that leaving Memphis had simply given me a much better chance to succeed in life. And it was also becoming clearer that a long overdue racial conflict was beginning to take form in the still decadent South.

CHAPTER EIGHT
ON TO YALE, THEN BACK SOUTH

There were about a thousand members of the Yale freshman class of 1959. Five of us were Negroes. I was the only one of the five who was from the South.

Some might have thought that being a Yale student would make a difference in the way I was treated in Memphis. That was not true, as reflected in a cynical riddle of the time:

Question: "Down South what do they call a Negro who leaves to better himself and get a great education and then returns home to try to do good?"

Answer: "That's easy. They call him a nigger!"

There was a sad truth in that riddle. Going to Yale did not mean that I was perceived differently by whites in the South, but rather that I came to perceive myself differently, no matter what anyone else may have thought.

The transformation was a gradual one. I was pleased to be going to Yale, but I have become much more deeply appreciative of Yale as the years have passed. In retrospect, it must have been one of the greatest days in my dad's life, though he never said it directly. He had not completed high school, but his son was fulfilling his dream by going to Yale!

And so it was that I became a student of the early sixties. It was the beginning of one of the most exciting eras of change in American history. My heroes became Martin Luther King, Malcolm X, Muhammad Ali, and Jack and Bobby Kennedy (the only white men I had ever seen stand up forcefully for the rights of Negroes).

In looking back on it, I have often asked myself what made Yale such a special place. For me it was the way in which students interacted. The dormitories were not like traditional dormitories. Most living units were suites with separate bedrooms and a living room. There were no corridors. The suites on each level opened into a common foyer which also had a full bathroom that opened into it. You shared the bathroom with your roommates and the other students in the suites on your floor. The importance of this physical arrangement is the interaction it fosters with your roommates as well as the other students.

In effect, Yale takes a diverse group of some of the brightest kids from America and around the world and puts them together in an intimate setting that allows them to grow and learn about life together. Much of what made it special was the exchange of ideas with other students in and especially out of the classroom. I learned how to listen as well as how to present my own views and ideas in the face of opposition from some of the brightest minds I would ever meet. Yale facilitated learning about life and formulating one's own views in a way I had never experienced before. In that environment, I was able to grow beyond the constraints of the racist South and to develop a different perception about people and a broader view of the world.

My freshman roommates were Ivars and Pete. Pete was from Dallas and was one of the most intelligent people I have ever met. Ivars' family was from Latvia, which I had never heard of. That is just a small example of Yale's diversity and the expansion of knowledge it fosters. Within a week, I had learned about Latvia, Lithuania, and Estonia and their relationship to neighboring Russia. I also learned how to drink vodka, another new experience. During the course of my college years, I also roomed with a Syrian, a Jew, a Pole, a New Yorker, and a white Southerner. The white Southerner, John, was not typical of the South. He was part Polish, part Jewish, and lived in Nashville. My interaction with my classmates at Yale opened to me a diverse, new world that would forever change my outlook. Pete and many of the others in my class were so bright that I began to focus some attention on the possibility that I just might flunk out of school. I thought about how deeply disappointed my family would be if I went to Yale and just was not good enough to make it. The fact that there were only five blacks in my freshman class made me feel even more pressure to be successful. Indeed, fear can be a great motivator, and I studied very diligently throughout that first freshman semester. The nice reward was that I made the

Dean's List; however, on the downside, my success also made me realize that continuing at Yale would not require me to study with quite the passion I had applied during that first semester. In my remaining three and a half years there, I opted for a somewhat less rigorous regimen. It included dating, alcohol, sports, and at least enough study to maintain what my colleagues in this lifestyle referred to as a "gentleman's average"—not too high, not too low, but just right—thereby allowing us the time to experience the other aspects of life.

I came of age at Yale in many ways, and especially because I entered at sixteen, two years younger than nearly all of my classmates. It was an experience I would not trade for anything in the world, even though I did not fully appreciate it until it was well behind me. It was there that I came to recognize the greatness in America that was in sharp contrast to the life I had been experiencing in the South. I also came much later to recognize the huge difference it had made in my life. On the recent occasion of our 50th reunion, I wrote this to my classmates in our reunion book:

> *"The experience of having spent four years at Yale profoundly influenced my life. The impact on me was in many ways greater than the impact on most of my classmates, because I was the only member of our class who was black and from the Deep South, Memphis, Tennessee. I grew up in Memphis, and hidden from my conscious awareness at the time was the enormous psychological impact of living in segregation. As the years have passed, I have become increasingly aware of how Yale affected my world view and how dramatically different*

that view likely would have been, if I had not had the privilege of attending Yale.

There is a sense in which living in a world in which you are continuously relegated to second class citizenship can strip away your self-esteem and self-confidence. It can also lead to a bitterness and sensitivity that, without intervention, could last for a lifetime. I can say thankfully, as we reach our fiftieth year since leaving Yale, that for me, Yale was that intervention. The contrast between Yale and the life I had experienced prior to coming to Yale created for me the vitally important realization of the essential goodness of mankind and the importance of living in a true democracy. However, it is only with the passage of time that I have come even more fully to appreciate these things.

My successes in my community from a business standpoint and from the standpoint of helping others are a by-product of those four years at Yale. It is not so much that I learned to be a better businessman or to be a better citizen. What I did learn is that there are good people in this world, that I feel fortunate to be able to count myself as one of them, and that good people with confidence, belief, and hope will persevere against whatever obstacles they may face. The years have shown me that we all face our challenges in life. What we do about them comes from within. Yale was the most important institution in my life in terms of instilling within me those qualities needed to maintain hope at all times and to persevere against whatever odds there may be.

Did I know this fifty years ago? Absolutely not. I was too carefree and cavalier to give it any real thought. I would have to say that I did not even know this ten years ago in the same way that I know it today. A turning point for me, unknown to me at the time, was a decision I made about a year ago to write a book. It was not the work of an author, which I have never been, but simply a desire to memorialize for myself those things that have been important to me in life. The title of the book did not come to me until I was more than halfway finished. It is simply this: One America: Moving Beyond the Issue of Race.

This is a book I could not have written, if I had not gone to Yale and had such great experiences with so many of you, my classmates. I doubt that I could have moved beyond the issue of race nor encouraged anyone else to do so. On this fiftieth anniversary I can truthfully say that the positivism and hope that were inculcated in me at Yale have indeed allowed me to move on in life, not merely with respect to race, but in so many different ways. And I am forever grateful for that."

My ever-increasing personal growth at Yale helped me endure the fact that each time when I returned home, the South was still the South. That cynical riddle about how educated Negroes were perceived became very clear to me during one of my summer visits to Memphis. I had turned eighteen a few months earlier, and Mother had taught me how to drive. Daddy didn't want to have any part of that, and now I can see his point. I think I inherited his impatience. Anyway, my mom taught me well, and I used the family car whenever I was in Memphis. During one afternoon of a summer vacation from college, I got the family car and picked up my girlfriend. We went to a local park and sat talking and watching the Mississippi River roll by.

Gradually, I became aware of the presence of a car pulling up next to us. This fellow in uniform got out of his car and asked: "Where you from?"

"We're from Memphis," I replied.

"Well," said the policeman. "What are you doing in this park?"

"We're just looking at the river," I answered.

"You can't look at it here," he said. "This park is for white people. You can go to a 'nigra' park."

We drove away. I had no wish to be arrested. The point was not lost on me that being a sophomore at Yale did not convey to me a right to sit peacefully in a Memphis park, because that particular park was for white people only. Indeed, I was back home again. But by this time I had seen and understood enough of life to realize beyond any doubt that something was terribly out of place in some parts of America. I had changed, but sadly, the South, like Old Man River, had just kept rollin' along.

CHAPTER NINE
AIR FORCE BLUES

I was neatly and crisply dressed in my Air Force blues and walking alone in the French Quarter in New Orleans. It was 1965 and I had volunteered for the United States Air Force Reserves. I was on leave from Lackland Air Force Base in Texas. I had heard about the excitement of New Orleans, and I decided to explore it for myself. I saw a bar and walked inside to buy a drink and a sandwich. The bartender saw me and said, "Sergeant, go outside and come over here to this window, and I'll take care of you right away." He was pointing to a small window toward the back of the bar.

My initial thought was that they must have some special deal for the military. "I will get to you first," he added. When I went outside, it was demeaning and demoralizing to me as a soldier to realize that what he meant was that Negroes were not allowed in the bar, but they could buy alcohol from a side window outdoors.

However, he was going to serve me first. That is, he was going to let me skip the line and get in front of all the other Negroes at the back window who were not in military uniform.

I went outside, glared at him momentarily and just kept walking. I never looked back. In that moment I came to a full understanding that I was never going to be willing to fight for America in the war zone in Vietnam. The reason was simple really. The war should have been in the American South, not South Vietnam, and it should have been over the freedom of Negroes in American society. That was the war I would have been willing to fight.

Fortunately, I was never called up to the war. And why indeed should I have gone and gotten shot at in Vietnam for a bartender who wanted to send me to the side window for Negroes in a country where too many, especially in the South, considered us to be second-class citizens? Let the bartender and his family fight in Vietnam for the status quo in which they had a much deeper vested interest than I did. I recalled what Muhammad Ali had said when he explained in very simple terms why he refused to be drafted: "I got nothing against no Viet Cong. No Vietnamese ever called me a nigger."[4]

The war in Vietnam was a dilemma for many of us who had recently graduated from college. I had graduated from Yale in 1963 when there was still a military draft. For a number of reasons, I did not believe in this war, but I also did not want to be a protester. Some young American men were beginning to go to Canada to avoid the draft. A few were openly burning their draft cards.

---

4 Muhammad Ali, 1967 – see reference for chiff.com

I was caught in the middle of all of this. I did not want to put my life on the line in a war that I believed was wrong. At the same time, I did not want to defy the federal government by becoming a draft dodger. Somehow, I stumbled upon a course of action that seemed right for me. In those days the military reservists were not called to war. It was a stateside based force that was rarely called to active duty, and even if called, the service was generally in the U. S., brief and pretty much risk free. I volunteered for the Air Force Reserves. I felt it was an honorable way out. It required six months of active duty (including several weeks at boot camp at Lackland Air Force Base near San Antonio, Texas), followed by a six-and-a-half-year commitment to report for active duty one weekend each month. Some cynically, and perhaps correctly, dubbed us as "weekend warriors." Nonetheless, we were in uniform, and we were serving our country.

Despite the way I personally felt, I also realized that there were many Negroes who held a different view and who wanted to fight in the war. I respected that. In the Negro community of that era, there was never the kind of divide over the war that engulfed the white community. The Civil Rights Movement may have fostered that division among whites. The movement made it not only right but, at least for some people, even honorable to challenge laws they deemed to be unjust. Many white kids seemed to embrace that concept more than Negroes did when it came to the military draft. The draft became a major focal point of a challenge to the status quo in America that I believe was the major dividing point between the liberal-leaning left and the more conservative right that has plagued the country ever since. Some families lost their sons and daughters in Vietnam while other families' children avoided the draft altogether. It must have seemed a cruel injustice for those who lost sons and daughters in the war to see draft dodgers who left the country return to America with full rights of citizenship.

The Negro community was different. There was some ambivalence about the war even among those who fought. Many recognized a hypocrisy in the attitude of a country that would send them to a war in Asia and then discriminate against them right here in America. Nonetheless, most were willing to fight.

A newspaper editorial I wrote reflected some of the inner conflicts Negroes felt about the war. I had begun writing a weekly article on the op-ed page in 1968 shortly after Martin Luther King was killed in Memphis. Prior to that time, the views of Negroes were simply absent from *The Commercial Appeal,* and the Negro community was protesting this exclusion as well as an insulting little Negro male caricature called Hambone that appeared regularly in the paper. Hambone was an affront to Negroes and was discontinued at about the same time the editor of the paper, Frank Ahlgren, hired me as the first Negro ever to write a column for the paper. I guess you could say I replaced Hambone in *The Commercial Appeal.*

The column I wrote reflected the outlook and attitudes of Negroes at the time. The following column about Negro soldiers returning from Vietnam was written in August, 1968.

Negro Soldiers: Do They Fight In Vain?

The Negro soldier has made a very significant contribution to the American war effort in Vietnam. He has fought and died in a greater proportion than the Negro constitutes in the general American population. Now many soldiers are returning from

Vietnam, and the black soldier must re-orient himself to this society.

Samuel Jeans is a 26-year-old Memphian who served in Qui Nhon in the 26ᵗʰ Transportation Company for one year. "I was determined to go there and do my job," he says. "Most of the guys there didn't want to be in a war, but I felt it was my duty to serve my country whether it meant life or death." This is not typical of returning servicemen, many of whom were disturbed by prejudice while in Vietnam, and especially by racial strife in America. Lewis Ford served 16 months in Vietnam as a squad leader in C Company of the 27ᵗʰ Infantry's Second Battalion. Of the racial difficulties at home, he said: "It got on your nerves a lot. I felt as though I was fighting in the wrong war."

A similar view is voiced by Frank Dilworth of 3030 Rochester, whose tour in Vietnam ended last December. "I felt bad not because of what they were doing in America, but because I couldn't participate," he says. As to whether his time in Vietnam was worth it, he says, "No, I've gotten behind in life. All that for nothing."

His attitude is fostered in part by the fact that since returning to Memphis, he has been unable to find employment. "While you're in Vietnam you think you are doing a good thing and maybe you'll get more breaks when you get back to the states by having served in Vietnam. But you don't. I think the man (the white man) just doesn't want to give any jobs to the brothers

(Negroes). A Negro guy feels bad coming back from Vietnam if he can't get a job in his hometown," he says.

This kind of disillusionment was also expressed by Charles Ford who is 23 and who served in the 124^(th) Transportation Company. "I haven't found a job since I've been back. I think I've been disillusioned a great deal. Once you're free of your service obligation, there is still a lot of trouble finding a good job."

Lawrence Becton of 3480 Millard has been one of the luckier returning Negro servicemen, for he was able to get his old civilian job at Hyman Building Company. "I came back and got the same job I had before. But there is discrimination as far as advancement is concerned," he says. He also feels that Vietnam is not sufficient cause for a war effort. "The reason I went is because of the consequences I had to pay if I didn't go. I was compelled to go," he says.

And so it is that the Negro veteran, after serving his time in Vietnam, returns to the same American society he left, a society in which he is unable to sustain himself simply because jobs are not available to him. This makes him bitter, because he feels that he has been through an ugly, bloody war all for nothing. He has been enough of a citizen to fight and die in war but not to live and work in peace.

For Samuel Jeans, however, the war did have some meaning. When asked if the war was worthwhile, he replied: "I can't say no. A friend very close to me died there. How can I tell his mother that it was all for nothing?"

Art Gilliam, The Commercial Appeal, August 5, 1968

Many Negro soldiers served honorably in Vietnam, and some made the ultimate sacrifice. It could be said that they were all heroes. It is a travesty that so many of those who returned home did not find a grateful nation waiting for them. They returned to a nation that offered them few jobs and often sent them to the side window. And what about those who returned in flag-draped coffins? It was a steep price to pay, when no Vietnamese ever called them a nigger.

CHAPTER TEN
WE'LL NEVER BE YOUNG AGAIN

One hundred years of delay have passed since President Lincoln freed the slaves, yet their heirs, their grandsons, are not fully free. They are not yet freed from the bonds of injustice. They are not yet freed from social and economic oppression. And this Nation, for all its hopes and all its boasts, will not be fully free until all its citizens are free.

-President John F. Kennedy, Televised civil rights address to the nation,
June 11, 1963

I will always remember the impact John F. Kennedy's televised 1963 speech on civil rights had on me. For every Negro in America that I knew, Kennedy represented hope. He was firm and outspoken in his view that all Americans, regardless of race, deserved fair and equal treatment. I had never before heard any white person speak in this way about the moral issue of fair treatment of Negroes. It was an inspiration and beacon of hope to me, and to Negroes throughout the nation, that the speaker was the President of the United States. During this era, in numerous Negro homes throughout America, when you entered the living room you would see three pictures on the wall: Jesus, Martin Luther King, and John F. Kennedy. Such was the esteem in which Negro Americans held this president.

When Kennedy was killed on November 22, 1963, I was sitting in a lecture on business law at the University of Michigan. The professor briefly interrupted his lecture and said, "I have just learned that President Kennedy was shot and killed in Dallas, Texas a short while ago." I don't remember anything else he said about the shooting. I do remember that he said he intended to continue his lecture, and he did. He seemed unaffected. I was appalled that he would think it was appropriate to keep lecturing. I guess when you've lived long enough and been jaded enough in life, there are few surprises, so you just keep on doing whatever you were doing. But I was only twenty years old and had not reached that level of cynicism, so I got up and walked out of the lecture hall with tears in my eyes.

As great as the despair was for Negroes when Kennedy was killed, I believe the impact on white Americans, especially the young, was even greater. Negroes had endured so much in America that it was difficult for any one disappointment, even one as profound as the Kennedy assassination, to impact our psyche any more than the innumerable injustices we had already suffered. But many white Americans, and in particular those young people who had been so fervent about Kennedy's election, had not experienced this kind of tragedy before.

There is simply nothing in the experience of the overwhelming majority of whites in America that would cause an awakening comparable to being a Negro in this country. The Kennedy assassination was one of two events in my lifetime in which white Americans were affected in a way that would provide even a remote semblance of the way Negroes had been affected by our experience in America.

In the aftermath of the assassination, *Washington Times* columnist Mary McGrory said to Daniel Moynihan of Kennedy's death, "We'll never laugh again." Moynihan, who was then Kennedy's Assistant Secretary of Labor and later became a senator from New York, replied to McGrory, "Mary, we'll laugh again, but we'll never be young again."[5]

The assassination had taken away the innocence of many white Americans in a way that was comparable to, but not as enduring or severe as, the racial awakening that had been experienced by Negro children. The age of innocence for too many of them is fleeting. Even those black children who are from a more recent generation are deeply impacted, through their parents and grandparents, by the attitudes and views of those who were exposed to the demeaning injustices of the past.

The second event in my lifetime that resulted in a comparable awakening from innocence for white Americans, especially for the young, was the attack on America by Muslim extremists on

5   Martin, Ralph G., *Hero For Our Time*, New York, Macmillan, 1983

September 11, 2001. That attack shook the sense of security and invulnerability of the American homeland that many had felt prior to the attack. The realization that a handful of terrorists could successfully attack America's greatest military symbol, the Pentagon, and one of its most important financial centers, the World Trade Center, on the same day was a frightening revelation for most Americans.

The Kennedy assassination and the 9/11 attacks brought with them a kind of collective psychological impact on those who were affected by them. In neither case was the impact as deep, or as profound, as the black experience in America. The similarity is that in each instance, there is a loss of innocence, and its effects can be profound. And it might well be said of those who experienced them that they will surely laugh again, but they will never be young again.

THE PSYCHOLOGICAL IMPACT

CHAPTER ELEVEN

A MATTER OF IDENTITY

My grandmother was born in 1895, and she always identified herself as colored. She never spoke of herself racially by any other term. When my mother, who was born in 1910, reached adulthood, she referred to herself as a Negro. My grandmother would just laugh at her whenever she called herself a Negro. Each generation took ownership of their particular label to the exclusion of all other labels, so it was amusing to my grandmother that her daughter called herself a Negro.

That irritated my mother to no end. "You're not colored, and stop calling yourself that!" my mom would say. My grandmother just kept laughing and would reply, "You're colored, too. You just don't know it." And in those early years both of them would bristle at being called "black." That term had a derogatory meaning. Its derisiveness stemmed from the fact that the blacker (darker complexioned) you were, the more you were looked down upon by the white society and therefore by those who were "colored" and those who were "Negro" as well.

I was born in 1943 and thereby became a part of the generation which, in young adulthood, came to identify itself as black. My mom hated that label and certainly did not find it humorous in the way my grandmother considered the term Negro. "Stop calling yourself black!" she admonished. I resisted the temptation to tell her she was black too and just didn't know it, but I continued to refer to myself as black. It was the term with which my generation described itself. I'm not even sure exactly when it came in vogue. I do know that in 1968, when the so-called godfather of soul music, James Brown, made a song about it ("Say it loud. I'm black and I'm proud."), most of us began to refer to ourselves as black if we had not already begun to use that self-identifier. Soul Brother Number One had made it not just acceptable, but important, to be black.

It became a clear statement of racial identity. It was an identity born out of a psychological adaptation to a white-controlled society in which we needed to be able to project ourselves as equals. Hence the term "black," the opposite and equal of white. That also meant it was an identity formed by contravention to the dominant white society in which we were still subjugated. In some ways "black" reflected anger more than a positive form of identity. Some blacks who were darker complexioned even began expressing disdain toward lighter complexioned blacks. Black standards of beauty began to change, especially on black college campuses where the reigning queens often became girls with darker complexions as opposed to the lighter skinned, whiter look.

The disillusionment this change must have wrought in fair complexioned women may have been offset by the new sense of redemption it afforded the darker skinned women. Clearly however, we had not all evolved to looking at the "content of their character." We had simply moved from overrating the importance of whiteness to now disparaging whiteness and elevating blackness in its place. This affirmation becomes a form of overcompensation in the quest for identity. Yes, I AM black. Yes, I AM proud. Yes, black IS beautiful (as if it hadn't been beautiful all along). All of this arose from the need to try to reverse low self-esteem with an overcompensating assertion of the importance of blackness.

The psychological aspect of the black experience in America was well captured in the writings of James Baldwin. Baldwin was one of the most insightful and widely read black writers during the racially turbulent 1960s. The poignant metaphor in his essay "A Fly in Buttermilk" is still relevant today, and it provides an excellent backdrop for an understanding of the psychological impact on blacks that derives from the American experience. The white buttermilk is overwhelming, inescapable, and ultimately suffocating. We are so engulfed in the pressures and too often the anguish of being black that, for most of us, race becomes the central factor in our outlook. The specific effect varies widely among individuals, but one common theme has been the ongoing need to answer the question, "Who am I?" While the search for identity may be common to most people of any race, for black Americans, due to our peculiar history, these identity issues are inextricably intertwined with race.

This search for identity is ultimately a consequence, directly or indirectly, of the effects slavery has had on black self-perception through the generations. There is one nearly universally consistent aspect of the black psyche that is an outgrowth of the American experience, and that is lowered self-esteem.

The esteem issue has manifested itself in various aberrations in black behavior. Many of them began when overt racism and segregation were so prevalent in America. These manifestations have mutated over the generations, but they are still recognizable today. Among the more apparent symptoms developed long ago as a consequence of the malaise of being black in America were the act of passing for white; the so-called HNIC (Head Nigger In Charge); and the "black bourgeoisie."[6] All exist today in some evolved form, and they are testament to the impact the racial history of America has had on the mind and spirit of black people.

In a segregated world, passing for white was a choice which very fair-complexioned blacks could make as to which racial life they would live—Negro or white? We were legally classified as "Negro" if we had a great-great grandparent who was Negro. In other words, if you had one-sixteenth Negro blood, then you were a Negro to the white society. We used to joke that Negro blood must be awfully potent, if one little drop of it can turn you into a Negro.

Under this definition, naturally there were many "Negroes" who looked white. Some even looked whiter than a lot of white people looked. Those who were very fair complexioned could remain in the black community where they were raised, or they could leave that community and quietly integrate themselves into the white community. It was called passing for white. Those who made this

6 E. F. Frazier, *Black Bourgeoisie*, New York: The Free Press, 1957

choice often forever left the community of their birth, and for all intents and purposes became white. The Negro passing for white accepted the benefit of being treated like a white person by society in exchange for the ever-unresolved psychological conflict of knowing within yourself who and what you really were. Such was the choice and dilemma of those who could pass for white and who chose to do so.

There were other Negroes who could easily have passed for white but who chose not to do so. They were often the ones who made sure they went all the way to the back of the bus so they would not be mistaken for being white. Those who made this choice continued to be faced with all the exclusions that beset Negroes in society, but perhaps they had a greater peace within themselves than those who chose to pass.

Joan was a high school classmate of mine who had the complexion of a white girl who had spent a good part of the summer at the beach. Her mom looked about as white as any white person you ever saw but never chose to pass for white. Her dad was tan and had relatively wooly hair, so he was not likely to be mistaken for a white person.

Joan had been shopping and was checking out at the cash register when the white checkout clerk said to her, "Girl, where did you get that beautiful tan?"

Joan smiled and replied, "From my daddy." There was a pause and a strange look from the clerk followed by a moment of awkward silence. It was the late 1950s, and in the Deep South you just weren't supposed to get your tan from your daddy!

Joan reflected both the hubris and the sense of humor of many of those who chose not to pass for white. She reveled in telling the story time and again, and every time she would laugh heartily at the stunned look on the white clerk's face. Joan chose to be a Negro and embraced it with all the anguish and exclusion that went with it. It was a circumstance she could have avoided simply by being someone other than herself.

Another interesting aberration in the search for identity was referred to by Negroes as the HNIC. It simply stands for Head Nigger in Charge. The expression itself illustrates the deep conflict, felt especially by Negroes who were egotists, between wanting so badly to be somebody and yet being relegated by society to the status of nobody. An HNIC was a Negro who had such a big ego that he made himself into a kind of caricature of a leader. He demanded to be the leader, and yet his inner insecurity was so obvious that other Negroes simply tolerated, and made fun of, his feeble attempts to demonstrate that he was indeed somebody. The HNIC embodied an impact of racism that made him akin to John Milton's fallen angel (the Devil) who found it "better to reign in Hell than to serve in Heaven."[7]

Too many of us, warped by society, wasted needless amounts of energy trying to be the HNIC by spending too much time on who would be in charge and too little time on life's real issues. Here we find the person who was happy in Hell so long as he could be the Devil, who is after all the HNIC of Hell.

---

7 John Milton, *Paradise Lost*, [1667], bk. I, l. 1

A third indication of behavior distorted by race was the emergence of the so-called black bourgeoisie. *Black Bourgeoisie* is a book first published in 1957 by E. Franklin Frazier. It is a study of the social world of the so-called Negro elite. They developed their own social world that reflected their misguided attempts to counteract the exclusions they faced in American society. They created a separate world of make-believe that became a neurotic facsimile of the social world from which they were excluded. Their fabricated society existed in a world of social isolation—isolation from the Negro masses that they rejected as inferior and isolation from the white world which refused to accept them. They professed racial pride, yet they mocked physical features associated with Negroes–broad nose, dark skin, and wooly hair. They were preoccupied with hair straighteners and facial whiteners.

They used their money to buy conspicuous displays of a higher standard of living in America. The black bourgeoisie reflect the fact that the black psyche can cause people to go to extremes to find acceptance. Frazier said, "The exclusion of middle class Negroes from participation in the general life of the American community has affected their entire outlook on life."[8] They are so involved with status that other things lose their perspective. And while there are also those in the general society who are obsessed with status, for the black bourgeoisie and their descendants this is an affliction born of the intersection of race with the longing for social status.

Passing for white, the HNIC, and the black bourgeoisie are just a few manifestations of the ways the matter of race has

---

8 E. F. Frazier, Op. cit.

been reflected in the black psyche. The inability to answer the question "Who am I?" is further reflected in continuing changes over the years in terms of how we have identified ourselves. First, we called ourselves "colored," then "Negroes," then "black," and more recently "African-American." It is not really clear when each moniker ended and the next one began to take its place.

Slavery is the central fact of American history that has given rise to the identity and self-esteem issues that have afflicted African-Americans. Unfortunately, both blacks and whites are in a form of denial about the insidious impact of slavery on modern day America. For whites it is much more convenient to simply relegate slavery to being a rarely discussed aspect of American history than to genuinely examine the enormous impact it continues to have on our nation. For blacks it is emotionally very difficult to introspect about the self-esteem issues that constitute the psychological legacy of slavery. Blacks and whites therefore, by and large, do not want to talk about slavery. Yet it is vitally important for all of us to understand its effects.

Regarding black self-esteem, various studies have been undertaken that have attempted to assess the self-perception of blacks. Scholars will debate, as I suppose they should, the accuracy and validity of particular studies. However, the only study we really need to consider in order to glean black self-perception is a study that was conducted for nearly three hundred years: African slavery itself.

The one simple fact we can all intuitively understand is that a master and a slave will have very different perceptions about themselves and about each other. Further, the psychological residuals of those perceptions will be carried forward for many generations to come.

Once we can accept that premise, we have the roots of the general psychological and behavioral differences between whites and blacks in America today.

It is significant to note that the first African-American president of the United States, Barack Obama, is not a descendant of the slaves. That does not mean he is any less African-American, nor does it mean that he is any less concerned with the future of black people in America. The significance of his heritage revolves around the self-esteem question. The President does not appear to have the self-esteem issues that reside, to a greater or lesser degree, in virtually all of the descendants of the slaves. While America was clearly ready for an African-American president, the country was probably not ready for an African-American afflicted with issues of self-esteem. Obama, as a child of African royalty and a white American mother, would prove to have a profoundly different sense of self than would be embedded in the psyche of the great majority of the African-American descendants of the slaves. That difference allowed Barack Obama to appeal to, and relate to, a wider range of voters.

Barack Obama has been a blessing to America. Whether one agrees or disagrees with his politics, this much is certain—his election helped the world see America in a new light. Perhaps even more important to our country, his election has helped African-Americans see themselves in a new light. Every child born in America today can genuinely be told that there is no limit to what he or she can become. A black child really can grow up to be the President of the United States. The one caveat is for that black child to fulfill this dream, he or she must first shed the deadweight of low self-esteem that has been our burden in America.

CHAPTER TWELVE
IF THERE IS A GOD

saiah's complexion was dark. He was very dark. He was much darker than most African-Americans. Isaiah was black in the way that very dark native Africans are black. In the Negro community of the mid-1960s and earlier, there was a term of mocking derision that some Negroes applied to people as dark as Isaiah. They were referred to as "dusty black." It was a time when Negroes were ashamed of their blackness. Their shame was a consequence of the continuous degradation and humiliation visited upon them. The darker you were, the lower your self-esteem was likely to be.

Isaiah had come to the University of Michigan Graduate School from rural Alabama. Nowhere in America was there more degradation from whites than was experienced in the rural South. In addition, Isaiah, being as dark as he was, was scorned by many Negroes as well. I met him after I had graduated from Yale, when

I was in graduate school at Michigan studying actuarial science (insurance mathematics).

Isaiah and I, along with three black undergraduates, were sitting together at a table in the student union. We were just exchanging ideas about a wide range of topics, when the conversation turned to religion. It was pretty common to talk about religion, especially in an academic environment in which there was such a diversity of beliefs and views.

"Is there really a God?" one of us speculated. "No one can prove there is a God," he added.

"I just want God to help me pass these frigging exams," said another.

The conversation went on briefly:

"I used to go to church, but I don't anymore."

"It's not that I don't believe in God. I go to church sometimes, but not the way I did when I was younger."

"I don't go at all, but I do pray sometimes."

It was a conversation typical of the times for students in an academic environment where freedom of thought and inquiry, even into so-called fundamental values, was encouraged. This was the sixties, and many values that had long been considered traditional were under scrutiny, especially on college campuses.

Isaiah had been silent. He was simply listening to the conversation. He was a highly articulate, intelligent fellow, and deeply introspective. Finally, he stood up and said: "There is no God! If there is a God, then why does he treat the black man so badly?"

The conversation at the table went still. None of us had an answer for that. It was the silence of consent with a point forcefully made. For Isaiah, there simply was no God. If you were dusty black and from rural Alabama, it was very easy to conclude that whatever God you may once have believed in had forsaken you. And since God is supposed to be a just God, then there must not be a God in light of the injustices heaped upon the black man. Indeed, if you were black from anywhere in America in the 1960s, it was apparent that Isaiah had asked a question that had no easy answer.

I had a sense that Isaiah would be forever trapped in his deep blackness. He may well have carried his hurt and disappointment with him for the rest of his life. In a very understandable way, he had been overwhelmed by the past. As Supreme Court Chief Justice Earl Warren had written in Brown v. Topeka, his "heart and mind had been affected in a way unlikely ever to be undone." What God would have allowed that?

CHAPTER THIRTEEN
BY WHATEVER MEANS NECESSARY

During the many decades of oppression, deeply Christian African-Americans often accepted their plight as part of God's plan. They believed there would be redemption in the sweet by-and-by. For others, traditional religion held no answers. How could there be a God when people were suffering the way the black man was suffering in America?

The Black Muslims in America (also known as the Nation of Islam) had an answer. There is a God. He is called "Allah." He will raise the black man in America from the clutches of Hell. It is not Allah who treats the black man so badly. It is the Devil. That devil is the white man in America. It is the white man who has wrongfully diminished the spirit of the black man. Allah will provide for the black man the path to redemption—not in the sweet by-and-by, but now!

That was the message. The Messenger was known to his followers as "The Honorable Elijah Muhammad." Racism in America had now given rise to a new black religion. It was a variation of Islam that had a powerful appeal to many blacks who had become so painfully downtrodden in America.

The Black Muslim movement was founded in Detroit in 1930 by W. D. Fard (known to some as Wali Farad), a silk salesman. Elijah Muhammad (originally Elijah Poole, born in Sandersville, Georgia) inherited the mantle of leadership when Farad disappeared in 1934. Farad taught that Christianity, which had forsaken black people, was not their true religion. Their true religion was Islam, the religion of the black peoples of Africa and Asia. The white man was the Devil, who had removed the black man from his native lands and enslaved him. The Devil had even taken the black man's name and forced him to adopt the surname of the white slave owner.

This message resonated very strongly with a number of blacks in America, especially those who were the most downtrodden and disenfranchised. It was a message that could help them redeem their lost self-esteem. It said, in effect, that black people were the exalted children of Allah and not the subservient lower class citizens they had become at the hands of the Devil. In embracing the Black Muslim movement, they shed their slave surname and replace it with an X, symbolic of their lost African tribal name, which might never become known to them. John Smith, for example, would become known as John X. In further reclaiming their true identity, Black Muslims must not only shed the slave name, but also such habits as drugs, smoking, and alcohol, which were perceived as being brought upon them as a result of their enslavement by whites.

The Muslim message had a special appeal to some who had reached the depth of depravation—pimps, prostitutes, criminals—many of whom were incarcerated. In a way, it was the perfect message for the redemption of oppressed blacks: you must disavow Christianity and claim your true religion; you must shed your slave name forced upon you by the white devil and adopt a new name; you must cleanse your body and mind and go forward with pride and hope, leaving behind the shell that has housed the degraded being you have become in America.

An imprisoned man named Malcolm Little became a convert to the Black Muslim faith. He was in jail in Massachusetts. In his days as a pimp and drug dealer, he had worn his reddish hair conked, as was the preferred fashion of many black men of that era. Conked hair was kinky hair that had been straightened by the use of a powerful chemical such as lye so that the hair came to emulate the straightness of the white man's hair. At that time many blacks tried to straighten their hair in some manner and to lighten their faces with facial lighteners that contained mercury. We were using chemicals to try to look like the white ruling class.

The Muslims taught that trying to become white was the exact opposite of what black people should be doing. We should instead embrace our blackness. The effectiveness of this message was directly attributable to the loss of black self-esteem that had been brought on by various forms of black disenfranchisement. Malcolm not only bought into the Muslim message as a prisoner in 1946 but became their chief spokesman not long after his release from prison in 1952. He had dropped the use of his slave surname, Little, and as Malcolm X, he became the most influential advocate for the Black Muslims in America for more than a decade. Malcolm's message reflected the Muslim belief in black nationalism and the ultimate separation of the black nation from the white population of the United States.

Malcolm was regarded as a militant. His contemporary, Martin Luther King, was seen by many blacks as more of a pacifist. In the rugged world of the black ghetto, Malcolm's message had more resonance. However, most blacks were not willing to convert to Islam. Over the generations, they had become much too rooted in Christianity to join the Black Muslims in massive numbers. Still, most blacks empathized with the message, though they might never become Muslims.

At the time, I did not perceive America as a nation that was likely to change through peaceful protest. I believed that Malcolm's militancy was more likely to lead to the liberation of black people than Martin's nonviolent approach. I had essentially lost confidence in the nation's ability to introspect and to rectify the injustices perpetrated against black people. But I was wrong. I had not considered that when you took into account the nation as a whole, a majority of Americans would become outraged at the repeated injustices that were taking place, especially in the South. What Martin Luther King was able to do was to shine the cleansing light of truth on these injustices so that they became clearer and more relevant to all Americans. He was thereby able to galvanize "people of good will" around a movement predicated on Mohandas Gandhi's strategy of nonviolence.

Blacks in the South understood all too well what the white man they were dealing with was capable of doing. However, millions of white Americans were oblivious to the depths of hatred and viciousness prevalent in the South. The Civil Rights Movement could never have been successful if whites had not empathized with it. It turned out that there were far more good white Americans who wanted to do what was right than there were bad white Americans who wanted to continue to subjugate blacks. Maybe one lesson in all this is that the good people greatly outnumber the bad ones, but that the bad people often make so much noise that they seem to comprise a majority. Too often the true majority is silent, choosing not to stand up against injustice until it becomes intolerably apparent. What Martin Luther King did, by appealing to the national conscience, was make it intolerably apparent. Malcolm's approach could not have done that.

What Malcolm did do was make it intolerable in the eyes of black people to continue to be devalued as human beings. He appealed to an instinct to fight for justice "by whatever means necessary." He confronted the system in a more militant way and appealed not to a nation's conscience but to the black man's sense of self. In his world, as he saw it in the early 1960s, the black man becomes the antagonist unwilling to accept his condition in life. King was more of a protagonist championing the rights of black men and women who were victims banding together to protest their station in life.

I do not believe Martin Luther King's approach prevailed because of its greater tactical effectiveness. Malcolm X may in fact have had the message with the greater appeal to black people. The reason Dr. King and his organization, the Southern Christian Leadership

Conference, became the standard bearer is simply because it was Christian. The black man in America had become too vested in Christianity over the centuries of slavery and oppression to gravitate in massive numbers to this new "alien" religion. To our enduring benefit as a nation, Christianity prevailed over Islam among American blacks. If it had not, the nation could have been irreparably and forever torn.

Thomas Jefferson would have been proven right when he said, "The two races, equally free, cannot live in the same government." The divide between a black Islamic America and a white Christian America would have had devastating consequences for the nation. Jefferson saw the irreconcilable nature of the nation's ideals and the realities of slavery. He foresaw the seemingly irreconcilable divide that would exist between whites and the freed slaves. Therefore he was right, except for one thing. What Thomas Jefferson did not foresee was that the nation he helped birth would one day produce Martin Luther King. Indeed, Malcolm had the message "by whatever means necessary," but King had the cross. To the nation's salvation, blacks chose the cross.

Black Muslim leader Malcolm X is shown addressing rally in
Harlem, New York on June 29, 1963. (AP Photo)

CHAPTER FOURTEEN
BLACK GLOVES RAISED HIGH

By the late 1960s, the spirit of protest against a predominantly white nation was widespread throughout the black community. Much of the protest, whether hostile or peacefully expressed, was offensive to whites who, to a great degree, could not understand the anger, because they had never been subjected to the circumstances that had led to that anger.

One particular protest that received international headlines was the demonstration by two black athletes at the 1968 Olympic Games in Mexico City. Tommie Smith and John Carlos were sprinters on the United States Olympic Team. Smith won the 200 meter race (gold), and Carlos came in third (bronze). A white Australian named Peter Norman was second and won the silver medal.

The two American athletes had planned their protest prior to the race. When the three athletes were presented with their medals at the Olympic Stadium, Smith and Carlos defied tradition by displaying symbols of the Black Power Movement in America. They both wore black socks representing black poverty. Smith wore a scarf around his neck representing black pride. Carlos wore a necklace of beads for "those individuals that were lynched or killed and that no one said prayer for . . . those who were thrown off the side of the boats in the Middle Passage [9] [the journey slaves made from Africa to the Americas aboard the slave ships]."

When the "Star Spangled Banner" played, Smith and Carlos each raised a fist covered by a black glove and bowed their heads, which was the black power salute in America.

Looking at the photo of the three athletes, it would be easy to conclude that the white athlete from Australia had unwittingly gotten caught up in this black demonstration. But that was not the case at all. Norman was very much aware of the planned protest. Smith and Carlos had each agreed to bring a pair of black gloves to the 200 meter race. However, Carlos had forgotten his gloves at the Olympic Village. It was Peter Norman who suggested that Carlos wear Smith's left glove. That is why Smith's right hand is raised in the traditional salute, but Carlos' left hand is raised instead.

Like Smith and Carlos, Norman wore a badge representing the Olympic Project for Human Rights. This organization had called for a boycott by black American athletes of the 1968 Olympic

---

9 John Carlos, 1968 – Wikipedia.org. 1968 Olympic Black Power Salute

Games. Although the athletes did not boycott the games, Norman was indeed sympathetic with the ideals of the organization and the views of the black American athletes.

Many Americans were incensed over the international "embarrassment" the country had suffered at the Olympic Games. But the protest was little more than a reflection of the fracturing relationship between America and its black citizens, a consequence of the psychological impact of all the years of degradation and exclusion. As they left the podium to boos from the crowd, Smith said, "We are black and we are proud of being black. Black America will understand what we did tonight." [10] He was right. They had spoken for black Americans. Smith and Carlos, while ostracized by the larger white community, were heroes in the black ghetto. At high school football games I attended that fall, hundreds of black teenagers raised their right fist when the national anthem was played.

However, that summer in Mexico City, the Olympic president, Avery Brundage, demanded that Smith and Carlos be suspended from the Olympic Games and expelled from the Olympic Village. There were many who saw an element of hypocrisy in Brundage's actions. He had been president of the U. S. Olympic Committee in 1936 when German athletes had made Nazi salutes during the Games. Brundage had not offered any objection to their actions. The alleged difference was that the Nazi salute was a national salute and therefore acceptable. But the salutes by Smith and Carlos were deemed to be individual salutes and therefore unacceptable. What Brundage and others did not recognize was that the salutes by

10 Tommie Smith, Ibid.

Smith and Carlos were a national salute. It was the salute of the protesting black nation that had been created within America.

During the next Olympic Games, there was yet another black protest. This time it was the subject of a column I wrote during the latter part of that Olympic year. The tone and focus of this column reflected the black attitude and spirit of the times:

Why Did Blacks Protest During Olympics?

The year was 1968 in Mexico City, and as the American flags were hoisted and the band struck up "The Star-Spangled Banner," two clenched black fists were raised skyward by the American Blacks who had finished first and third in the 200 meter run at the Olympics.

Tommie Smith and John Carlos embarrassed the United States with their dramatic protest, and they were suspended from the team and ordered to leave the Olympic Village—a lesson to dissuade future demonstrators.

Now, four years later, the scene is Munich, Germany. Again, American flags and the national anthem salute two black sprinters, first and second in the 400 meter run. This time there are no clenched fists; there is instead a casual air of almost total indifference. And once more America is embarrassed before the eyes of the world.

Many Americans disparage the actions of this year's sprinters, Vince Matthews and Wayne Collett. But should one attempt to judge whether a man is right or wrong for failing to respect protocol? I think not. It seems to me such questions as: "Should they have protested?" or "Should they have been penalized for protesting?" are really illusory and quite separate from the real issue.

There is only one basic issue in both the 1968 and the 1972 demonstrations by America's black Olympic athletes. That issue is why some of the nation's most talented young blacks place their race before their country.

The fact that race comes before country for these men was clear even before the 1972 Olympics had begun. America's black athletes threatened to boycott the games in sympathy with black Africa over the presence of racist Rhodesia at the Olympics. At that point the black members of the American team clearly had placed race before country, and the subsequent indifference they showed at the awards stand really should have been no surprise.

The real issue then is WHY these men feel as they do and not WHETHER they should feel this way. And if you will face that issue squarely, you will arrive at the very unpalatable truth, which is that their country has served more to reinforce their allegiance to race than their allegiance to country.

American blacks have absolutely nothing in common with black Africans except race. There are no cultural ties; no social bonds; we cannot even communicate with each other linguistically. Yet American blacks feel this allegiance to the Africans.

What does this mean, America? It means that you have forced upon us an identification with skin color that transcends language, cultural and social barriers—that spans 4,000 miles of ocean and links us with Africans with whom we have only skin color in common. You have made us not black Americans, but American blacks. BLACK is the noun, and being an American is only an adjective which slightly modifies that noun. White America, you and you alone have made it so. Don't knock us now for what you have made us feel during a concerted effort of 350 years of oppression.

It is extremely difficult for me to understand why white people can't seem to realize that an American flag doesn't mean the same thing to blacks that it means to whites. Does the flag of a slave ship mean the same thing to the slave that it means to the captain? That's not to say that contemporary America is analogous to slavery (although that is obviously part of this country's history), but the principle is very much the same. That is, the stars and stripes take on a little more meaning when you have a steak on the table in your own home with a two-car garage than when you are hungry, cold, and have no place to go.

When will American blacks stop embarrassing America before the world community? As soon as America stops relegating blacks to a lesser station in society. As soon as America gives us a vested interest in those things to which all this protocol is addressed.

So to those who say the athletes are wrong, I say it is America which has been wrong. The actions of its black athletes are simply manifestations which you may not happen to like. And if you don't like them, the best thing to do is work toward a 1976

when today's American blacks can feel like black Americans
and be proud to stand at attention before an American flag.

Art Gilliam, The Commercial Appeal, *September 25, 1972*

In 1968 when these protests first began, Tommie Smith and John Carlos were ostracized in America for their actions during the Olympic Games. Peter Norman was likewise shunned by many in his native Australia. He was denied an opportunity to participate in the 1972 Olympics even though his performance in the trials would have normally earned him a place on the team. Eventually, Norman fell on hard times, and he died in October, 2006. Two of the pallbearers at his funeral were Tommie Smith and John Carlos—the final farewell in a friendship formed at the 1968 Olympic Games in Mexico City between two protesting black athletes and a white Australian who understood their cause.

In this Oct. 16, 1968 file picture, extending gloved hands skyward in racial protest, U.S. athletes Tommie Smith, center, and John Carlos stare downward during the playing of the Star Spangled Banner after Smith received the gold and Carlos the bronze for the 200 meter run at the Summer Olympic Games in Mexico City. Australian silver medalist Peter Norman is at left. (AP Photo)

LETTING GO OF THE PAST

CHAPTER FIFTEEN
THE LONG SHADOW OF SLAVERY

Idon't remember that we ever talked about slavery at home when I was growing up. It was never discussed in school either, even at the all-Negro school I attended. Looking back on it, slavery was, in a way, conspicuous by the fact that it was not mentioned. However, its psychological impact was pervasive down through the generations.

My mother's great, great grandmother was born around the time slavery was ending, yet slavery's influence on my mother was clear. "She's a nice girl, but she's so dark," she said, referring to a girl I was dating in college who was brilliant and truly a gem as a person. Her relatively dark complexion was a negative in Mother's mind, because dark skin was regarded by her, and many others of her generation, as an unattractive trait. That notion stems directly from African slavery. The slaves were largely very dark-skinned, and they were relegated by whites to an underclass without certain basic human rights. Therefore, the physical characteristics of the slaves would be perceived by them and their descendants as inferior characteristics, and the vestiges of those feelings of inferiority would last for many generations to come.

My mom did not want me to date anyone who was too dark by her standards. Yet she felt a distinct unease if I was dating a white woman. I think it was partially her sense of inferiority to whites as well as her inability to communicate easily with them. The lack of communication would make it very difficult to hold those little chats that mothers invariably want to be able to have with their son's girlfriend or wife. She also feared what might happen to me in a society where, at the time, interracial dating was uncommon. So it was quite an interesting afternoon when some time after I had finished college, I took a white girl over to meet Mom. By this time, my dad had passed away, and I called her to tell her we were coming to see her. She had never met Susan and did not know she was white—until she opened the door!

I was surprised that Mom carried on the conversation as if she had not noticed a thing. We stayed about half an hour and not once did she give even the slightest inkling that she had any unease or concern. I left believing that I had simply underestimated her and that she had somehow become this liberal, accepting person whom I was meeting for the first time. In reality, she was simply so stunned that she didn't know how to react. I stopped by her house alone later that evening.

"Art, why in the world didn't you tell me that girl was white?" she asked, incredulous that I would not give her advance warning.

"Well, I knew you'd figure it out," I replied casually, laughing under my breath.

She just shook her head in disbelief and went on about her business without another word.

Her fears and concerns about my dating Susan, as well as her virtually opposite concern that some black women were too dark for her son, were both by-products of slavery three generations removed. The simple truth is that African slavery is the most central underlying element in the race issue in this country between blacks and whites. If Kunta Kinte[11] and millions of other Africans like him had not been forcibly brought to these shores, it is not likely that there would have been any significant black presence in America, and there would be no racial issues to discuss. The American dialogue on race therefore needs to begin where the race problem began—with slavery.

As a nation, we must be willing to confront and accept that part of our history if we are to effectively begin to understand the relationship between blacks and whites in America. Accepting slavery means openly embracing it as an integral part of American history without any associated emotional impact or ethical judgments. This embrace of slavery as a vitally important historical fact needs to be complete, to the point where we can talk about it and analyze it objectively and understand how it has impacted America.

---

11 Alex Haley, *Roots: The Saga of an American Family*. Doubleday, 1976. Kunta Kinte was the name of an African from The Gambia kidnapped and brought to America as a slave.

The facts about slavery are pretty simple and straightforward considering the enormity and complexity of the impact it has had. African slavery in America began in the 1600s and it continued at such a pace that by 1860 there were four million slaves in America. They had been shipped from Africa with no return address. Their lives and culture, as they had known them in their native Africa, were stripped away never to be restored. The 1977 television series "Roots," based on the novel by Alex Haley, might more appropriately have been entitled "Uprooted." The impact of slavery was so pervasive that for two hundred years, the Africans brought in bondage to this country, and most of their descendants, knew nothing but slavery in America.

One reason African bondage persisted for so long was its enormous value to the country. It could literally be said that much of America's wealth and power was built on the backs of the slaves. By 1860 slaves had become the nation's largest single financial asset. They were worth more than $3.5 billion in 1860 dollars—"more than the value of America's railroads, banks, factories, or ships," according to an article in *Time* magazine.[12]

The nation fought the bloodiest war in its history over slavery, because the values of the founding fathers expressed in the Declaration of Independence "that all men are created equal" came into irreconcilable conflict with the Constitution of the new Confederacy of the South: "Our new government is founded on exactly the opposite idea; its foundations are laid, its cornerstone rests, upon the great truth that the negro is not equal to the white man; that slavery, subordination to the superior race, is his

---

12 David Von Drehle, "The Civil War: 1861-2011," *Time*, April 18, 2011.

natural and normal condition,"[13] said Confederate Vice President Alexander Stephens.

This feeling of white superiority, especially among white Southerners, persisted down through the generations much as the feelings of inferiority projected onto blacks persisted. An experience I had with a white corridor-mate in graduate school in Ann Arbor, Michigan in the mid-1960s brought the attitudes of certain white Southerners more clearly into focus.

"Rabbit" was from South Carolina. He had talked about how much he liked going to the Bahamas, and he bragged about the sex he had with Bahamian women. He went with me a few times to a black nightclub in Ann Arbor, and on one occasion, after a few drinks, he pinched the black waitress on the butt while laughing and giggling about it. The waitress was very agitated, turned to me and said with a glare "You think it's okay for him to pinch me, but you go to a white club and pinch a white waitress and see how he reacts!" I didn't respond. I did not think what he did was okay; I just did not do anything about it. I thought he had gotten too high and acted inappropriately, but I just did not put it in a racial context. A couple of months later, Rabbit's actual racial attitude became clearer.

My roommate from Boston fixed me up on a blind date with a blonde-haired white girl. We continued to date for a while, and at times, when my roommate was away, she stayed overnight in the dorm. It was not uncommon on the corridor for dates to sleep over. Most of the other white guys on the corridor, who were primarily

13 Ibid.

from the East or the Midwest, seemed okay with the relationship. However, Rabbit couldn't handle it. He stopped communicating with me, and told one of the other guys, "Rabbit just doesn't go for that."

Some of the others saw the irony in his bragging about sex with natives in the Bahamas and pinching the black waitress on the rear end yet having a deep problem with a black man being involved with a white woman. Over time I came to realize that this was a part of the sense of entitlement shared by many white men, especially from the South. They believed it was fine to do whatever they wanted to do with black women, but could not accept black men dating white women. Indeed, more than one Southern politician has been found to have had his hand in the cookie jar while at the same time being a staunch advocate of racial separation and discrimination.

For some of us, the hypocrisy in that might seem stunning, but for those politicians and others who believe in this double standard, it is probably for them just a part of the natural order of things. An aspect of this attitude is also rooted in general male chauvinism, but that is another subject. For now, the issue is simply that a significant part of the way we perceive race, black and white alike, derives ultimately from the legacy we inherited from the institution of slavery.

There are no easy answers to how we can address this continuing problem in our society, but one thing is certain. We need to embrace the reality of slavery and acknowledge as a nation that there really is no such thing as free labor. Someone pays the price somewhere and at some time.

We are today still paying the enormous cost of the slave trade. As a society, we must connect the dots, between the slavery of yesterday and the black crime and incarceration rates today, between the slavery of yesterday and the black poverty rate today. The role of slavery in our history has contributed heavily not just to the incidence of crime and poverty, but to the lack of education, to poorer health outcomes, and to so many other factors that comprise the disparities in our society between blacks and whites.

What most white Americans are more likely to acknowledge is the level of opportunity that many African-Americans now have and the notable progress they have made in American society.

That is true, and it is a fact that should be embraced by all of us, black and white alike. But it is not enough to look at only the brighter side of the American story. We must also embrace with equal fervor its darker side. But we don't like to introspect, personally or as a society, to the point of acknowledging these uncomfortable truths for which we must then hold ourselves accountable. The uncomfortable truth is that America today is still paying a price for slavery.

How do we get past this? There is a black component and a white component as to how we need to move on. Both involve a dispassionate acceptance of history.

African-Americans must understand and accept that there are facts of history that may seem wicked, cruel, and even evil. It is very difficult to let this go in order to begin healing the psychological effects it creates. However, we must realize that this is *history*. It is done. It cannot be undone. Slavery is a historical fact that has no emotion in and of itself. Any associated emotion is what we ourselves bring to it. We have to get over it, a terribly formidable task not easily accomplished, but very necessary. What has happened to virtually all of us, to a greater or lesser degree and largely hidden from ourselves, is that our self-esteem has been compromised.

One example that comes to mind involves a close friend who was engaged to a great guy. She was medium brown in complexion and he was a bit darker than she was. Of special concern to her was that his mother was much darker than he was, and she wondered if the mother's darker genes would then be passed on to her children, thereby making them darker than was acceptable for her. She seemed more concerned about whether she would have darker babies than whether she would have healthy babies. It was as if she would like to have an amniocentesis to test for the unborn child's skin complexion in the way that other families might want to test for Down's syndrome.

This kind of relatively subtle consequence of slavery goes unseen by most black people in America in the same way that the world seems darker when we look at it through sunglasses. Too many of our people are wearing these "sunglasses" within ourselves that distort the world around us. The dimming lens of low self-esteem colors that world. When our world seems dark, we too often believe that this is just the way the world is. In reality our lowered self-esteem is the unseen pair of sunglasses through which we perceive that world. The world is not as dark or as sinister as we may believe it to be.

Most whites also simply do not perceive slavery's relevance to America today, or they want to avoid the discomfort of discussing it, or both. It is not easy to make the connection between slavery and issues in today's society that are racial in nature. In America we are generally not taught to think like historians. We are more of a "now" society. Too many whites see the obvious problems that exist in black communities as self-generated. These problems are looked upon more in the context that black people have the same opportunities as white people in America, and therefore the failure to capitalize on these opportunities comes from within "those people." Any historical context is regarded as essentially irrelevant. It becomes easy to think of slavery as something that was long ago and far away and that has no effect on America today. This unfortunate and incorrect viewpoint is buoyed by the fact that there are obviously many dramatic black success stories in America.

But the success stories do not tell the whole story. It was very disconcerting to me, in discussing with white associates the fact of discrimination in this country, to hear a retort like "You went to Yale; therefore, there is no discrimination in America." Today, it is even worse: "Barack Obama is President; therefore, there is no discrimination in America." In that sense, electing our first African-American president, as important as it was in reflecting how far we have come, could have the unfortunate effect of creating the illusion that somehow our racial problems are behind us.

These successes can thereby become part of the reason that the strong vestiges of slavery become obscured. We need to think of slavery, and the insidious discrimination and hatred that came after it, as a fish net cast around the slaves and their descendants. Like any fish net, it did not restrain all of the fish. But make no mistake about it, the net cast by slavery, and its aftermath, still looms ominously in the waters of American society today.

White Americans must come to understand that recognizing the impact of slavery on our nation does not involve making a moral judgment about America today. We cannot subject ourselves in this country to some sort of white guilt trip about slavery. It happened. It is over. It took place many generations ago. Further, it requires no apology. It simply needs to be accepted, which means recognizing its implications for the America we live in today.

This is not to suggest that an apology is a bad thing; it is just not the most important thing. What is important is recognition of how slavery impacts us today and how it affects race relations in America nearly one hundred and fifty years after the Emancipation Proclamation. Black and white people in America have an awful lot of work to do to improve race relations. For African-Americans it is not easy to recognize, let alone acknowledge, the extent to which our world is being seen through dark glasses of which we are unaware. We are more apt to deny that our self-image has been impacted in ways that influence our daily actions and reactions than we are to take ownership of this lingering effect of slavery.

Likewise, white Americans need to realize that slavery is not over in terms of its impact on the nation today. Just as no discussion of how America became the great free nation it is can be fully informed without understanding the importance and impact of the Revolutionary War, so also can no discussion of race relations in America be fully informed without understanding the importance and impact of the long shadow of slavery.

Reconciling race in America is a very difficult task. There is no simple solution as to how it can be done. But it needs to be done, because we are all bound to a common fate. There can be no such thing as one outcome for white America and a separate outcome for black America. There can only be one outcome for one America. The truth is that whereas many of our white ancestors arrived on these shores aboard pilgrim ships like the *Mayflower* and many of our black ancestors arrived on these shores aboard slave ships like the *Armistad*, one thing is absolutely certain. Fate has placed us all in the same boat now.

WHERE BLUEBIRDS FLY

Our history of slavery and its ongoing impact have created psychological issues for nearly all blacks who have grown up in America. However, it is not easy to recognize some of our own issues, because we are not able to look objectively at ourselves. We can only look from within ourselves at the world outside. It is therefore difficult to know when our lens is out of focus.

A motivational seminar I attended many years ago crystallized much of this in my mind, even though the speaker's intention in telling the story was somewhat different from the message I took from it. He recounted a story of a very small puppy that was chained to a tree with space to roam around the tree but no ability to move outside that circle. This condition persisted until it grew to an adult dog. At that point the chain was removed, but the dog continued to remain within the confines of the circle. The speaker's point was that we need to get outside our comfort zones if we are to fully express ourselves and relate to the broader world around us. We should not confine ourselves within the limits of our circles.

To me this analogy was also fully applicable to the effects of slavery. The dog was free, but the dog's mind was not free. Similarly, the slaves, though unshackled, were still slaves in their own minds and retained the extremely low regard for self one would fully expect a slave to have. That lack of esteem has been passed on to generation after generation.

It was not easy for me to recognize my lowered self-esteem, let alone try to overcome it. A book I read during that time helped me come to a better understanding of how I had been affected psychologically by the innumerable instances of discrimination and exclusion I had faced for so long. The book was *Psycho-Cybernetics*[14] by a plastic surgeon named Maxwell Maltz. An example he gave struck a chord with me that created a new awareness, which started me on a long journey of greater self-discovery. He made the observation that two people might have opposite reactions to the same reconstructive surgical outcome, reactions governed not so much by the result of the surgery but by their self-perception prior to the surgery. A person with low self-esteem might still feel quite ugly even after very successful plastic surgery. A more beautiful nose, he explained, did not mean a more beautiful self-perception.

Maltz went on to give an example of how two people with nearly the same scar held opposite views of their disfigurement. One

---

14 M. Maltz, *Psycho-Cybernetics*, Prentice-Hall, Inc., 1960

of them desperately felt a need for plastic surgery to remove the shameful scar. The other was so proud of the scar that plastic surgery would not only be undesirable but, if performed, might actually result in a lowered sense of self. One of the two people, in what I found to be an eye-opening example, was a young woman who had been in a car accident that resulted in a scar on her cheek. She was ashamed of the scar and wanted to hide it. The other person, who had quite a similar scar, was a member of a German fencing society. His scar was for him a badge of honor incurred in battle and displayed with pride as a symbol of his courage. They had the same scar but totally different perceptions of it. It connected with me in terms of an almost instant realization that the "scar" of racial identity had generated in me more of the attitude of the accident victim than the attitude of the fencer.

I came to recognize that despite my accomplishments in life, being relegated to the back of the bus, feeling the impact of the murder of Emmett Till, being denied access to public places, and scores of other such signals I had experienced early in life, and throughout my life, had wounded me deeply in terms of self-perception. Maxwell Maltz's book helped me understand that I had to somehow let go of these adverse influences from my past. His example of the opposite reactions of two different people to their scars helped me come to the vital recognition that the scar of race had no objective meaning in and of itself. Its meaning would be whatever I believed it to be. That began a journey where I was letting go the adverse influences of the past and living more in the present. Over time, the past no longer had as much effect on my psychological well-being.

There is no one right way, or even best way, that I know of for taking this journey. You can't just type it in your computer like we do with MapQuest and get instant directions from here to there. Nor will it come through a sudden revelation. It is a process. What may come as a revelation is the fact that we are trapped in our history and have a need to begin a journey to psychological freedom. One thing that helped on my journey was coming to understand just how much people everywhere have in common. I recalled that Martin Luther King once referred to death as life's great common denominator. I also think that our urge to survive, to do well, to see our families do well comprise another common denominator that we share to a significant degree. The more I have come to know an ever-widening, diverse array of people, the more I have come to understand how much we really do have in common, even when we don't realize it. It helps overcome low self-esteem to understand that people are, in the final analysis, not so very different from each other.

One of my most difficult challenges was becoming comfortable with dating white women. At the time I was growing up, in the South and maybe everywhere, it was a huge taboo in the majority white society for black men to date white women. The taboo did not apply in the same way to white men being with black women; however, black men had been lynched in parts of the country for being even suspected of approaching a white woman romantically. That is probably one reason I felt uncomfortable dating white women even though some of my more liberal white classmates were quite eager to fix me up with dates who were white, especially since there were so few black women in our academic environment. Some of them thought it would be really cool for me to date a white woman, but it made me nervous, which was not cool at all. I found myself feeling a little insecure dating white women, although I did become more comfortable over time. All in all though, due to my insecurities, it was a pretty lonely social life.

One aspect of the modern dating scene helped put interracial dating in perspective for me more than anything else. It was Internet dating. I ventured into Internet dating before it was really as accepted as it eventually became. At that time, people might look at you with some degree of skepticism about your social skills if they considered that you had to go to the Internet to find a date. The way I looked at it was that it beat the heck out of going to a bar. Besides, what would you really mainly find at a bar other than a bunch of inebriated guys? Furthermore, the Internet offered thousands of choices, far more than even the largest church or college campus or wherever else I might think of as a place to meet women. It also gives you the chance to indicate your preferences, and I left mine wide open. I did not specify race, religion, nationality, or most of the things you could specify in the person you were seeking. In effect, I had placed myself in a race-neutral dating environment. The result was that I ended up dating women from various places around the world, including Germany, Israel, Taiwan, and Denmark. The most frequent matches were white and American, many of whom were from California and Florida. On one occasion, I was walking down the street in Sausalito, California with Jolie, whom I had met on the Internet, and she mentioned something that I had not observed.

"Have you noticed that some of the people we pass on the street are kind of staring at us?" she asked.

"No, I haven't noticed that at all," I replied.

"I think they are not used to seeing an interracial couple," she added.

She did not really care. She was just making an observation, but what I instantly recognized was that I had gotten beyond the sense of being uncomfortable dating women who were white. I felt just as comfortable as I had always felt with black women. It was an enormous change that had simply evolved with time and familiarity.

Some months later I met Dorrit on the Internet. Her home was in Copenhagen, Denmark. We exchanged emails and talked on the phone for several weeks before I invited her to come to Memphis. She had been to America a few times, but never to the South. I did not even consider the fact that she was white. I just invited her. Over the course of the next few months she visited several times, and we got married exactly one year after we first met on the Internet. This year we celebrated our ninth wedding anniversary.

Her outlook and attitude have helped me move even further along the road to more positive self-discovery. We were traveling through Mississippi by car on the way to Florida. Mississippi has indeed changed a lot from the days of deep racial prejudice and hatred directed at blacks by whites. However, we stopped at a convenience store in a relatively small, rural town where interracial couples seemed to be frowned upon, to say the least. A couple of women at the counter really glared at her in a very condescending way. She just looked at them and smiled her very lovely and friendly smile.

"And how are you ladies today?" she said as she made her purchase and walked out of the store.

That kind of exceptional ability to avoid getting caught up in the negativity of the moment helped me with my own introspection.

Eventually on my journey of self discovery and overcoming the past, I came to have the good fortune of being able to enjoy my successes and not allow my failures to diminish me. We all have our share of both success and failure. Unfortunately, failure or the perception of failure can undermine self-esteem because we often take our failures personally and don't put them in perspective. When I was a young boy, I once cried almost uncontrollably because I struck out in a baseball game. I felt that I was a failure because I was not able to hit the ball. We have to come to the point of having enough confidence to realize that even though we may *fail* in a particular effort, it does not make us a *failure*. That rather small grammatical difference makes a huge difference in terms of self-perception.

One day a few years ago, after I had come to have a better and much more positive sense of self, I noticed there was a song lyric I had begun to repeat to myself over and over. It had happened spontaneously, and I wasn't even sure just when it had begun. The song was "Over the Rainbow" by Edgar Harburg from "The Wizard of Oz." The well-known lyric tells of how bluebirds fly over the rainbow. Indeed, I was thinking that since birds fly over the rainbow, then as the song suggests, we too can rise spiritually even above our rainbows.

I think for all of us there awaits a place where bluebirds fly and where we can truly feel free and happy. Sometimes to get there, we must let go of certain aspects of our past. For virtually all blacks in America, race is the main issue we must put in perspective. In general though, many people have some parts of their past that need to be put aside so they can ascend over their rainbow.

CHAPTER SEVENTEEN
ENTITLEMENT AND ARROGANCE

One day in an advanced mathematics class at the University of Michigan, I was doodling somewhat inattentively when the professor, also head of the mathematics department, asked the class the solution to a problem. He had written quite a lengthy set of equations on the blackboard, but no one in the class could come up with the mathematical culprit that was obscuring the solution. I did not offer a possibility. I was still doodling. When it was clear to him that no one had the answer, he made this proclamation about the impediment.

"The nigger in the woodpile here is . . . . .!"

I was the only black person in the class, and I must say that he got my undivided attention with that remark. I did not say anything about it during the class, but I later sent him a note expressing how deeply offensive the remark had been. He wrote back embarrassed and apologetic. I remember that he pointed out how sometimes our mind plays tricks on us. I think he was genuinely regretful. He seemed almost like a savant who was so totally focused on math that he had used the word "nigger" without any real consideration of the true effects and implications of its use. But savant or not, I did not return to the class again except to take the final exam. I went back for the exam only because I did not want to allow this man and his comment to keep me from getting my degree. To be fair to him though, I think he graded the exam pretty generously.

The professor's remark was more than merely politically incorrect. It reflected an insensitivity and lack of awareness shared by many whites in America, especially men. Many white men exhibit an attitude that may not be racist or sexist per se but that comes across as a feeling of entitlement and arrogance. Many of them have been raised from birth to believe that they are simply entitled to opportunities and advantages because of who they are. On the surface, this kind of "optimism" may not seem problematic. But that is an illusion, because beneath the surface such an attitude gives rise to an ethnocentricity that is a form of prejudice. It may not be the kind of insidious prejudice wherein one seeks directly to deprive others. It is a different kind of prejudice: where one believes, deep within, that those who are not like him are not as capable as he is—as if those who are different do not deserve a seat at the Round Table.

Some might call it *chutzpah*; or perhaps *cojones*; or just simply hubris. By any name, it projects the misplaced notion of entitlement over women, blacks, gays, Latinos, Muslims, and pretty much anyone else who is not perceived to be worthy. This attitude of white male entitlement must be left behind if America is to realize its full potential in today's world. This country is no longer the kind of overwhelmingly white male dominated society it once was, and it never will be again. Yet white males remain by far the most influential demographic group in America. The nation will decline both internally and internationally, as long as white males continue to view the country and the world through this prism of entitlement.

We do live in a great nation. If we did not, blacks would still be slaves; women would still be without voting rights, and so on. The framers of the principles on which America was founded had a vision that has brought us this far forward to become the greatest nation on earth. They may well have reckoned that someday the country would have to deal with its pluralism. Based on Jefferson's comment noted in the prologue to this book, he certainly knew that something would have to be done about the slaves other than continued slavery. The time is upon us now for our nation to fully embrace our diversity, or we could well be supplanted in the role of world leadership by more homogenous societies that do not have to spend energy resolving diversity. Today in this great symphony we call America, many instruments are out of tune. We show too little respect for the rights, views, appearance, and orientation of others. But we do have a choice. We can play in tune with each other with a harmony that transcends our differences and energizes us collectively. In harmony, America can truly move mountains. Or we can choose to play out of tune in a discordant medley of hatred, bigotry, and envy. And rather than conquering mountains, we will only erect new barriers.

If we keep fighting each other and fail to fully embrace and respect the rights of others, America's rich diversity could become America's Achilles' heel.

At the core of embracing diversity is for blacks and whites in America to come together. Given our history, if these two races can unite in a spirit of unity and brotherhood, then all Americans should be able to come together, and America will then truly demonstrate to the world that pluralism can work on this fragile planet. In that context, the Emancipation Proclamation is almost equal in importance to the Declaration of Independence. No nation that proclaims liberty and justice for all can really be free while holding millions in slavery.

The writ of independence may have marked our birth as a nation in 1776, but the end of slavery in 1863 declared us truly free; slaves were no longer prisoners in America, and America was no longer a prisoner to its own internal conflict.

Picture an America where blacks have a positive self-image and thereby fewer of the antisocial tendencies that plague our society. Picture an America in which whites, and especially white males, fully embrace diversity so that every American has a genuine stake in our success as a nation. That is the America which can truly be a beacon to the world. That is the America whose lamp shines beside the golden door.

ONE AMERICA

CHAPTER EIGHTEEN
THE FRONT OF THE BUS

One day I was walking on Second Street near downtown Memphis. I don't remember the year, but I was in my thirties. A Memphis city bus had stopped at the red light at Second and Vance. The bus driver honked his horn at me twice to get my attention, and when I looked up at him, he waved at me. After a moment of looking at him very closely, I realized it was Aaron, one of my classmates from Hamilton High School whom I had not seen in more than twenty years. At Hamilton, Aaron and I and all of our classmates had to ride in the back of the bus. And here was Aaron not only riding in the front of the bus but driving the bus! What a sea change! He was one of an early group of several black bus drivers. Such change as this reflects the capacity of a democracy to correct its course over time.

What became even more significant to me, especially given the history of Memphis, was that in 1993 a black man named Will Hudson became the president and general manager of the bus company, Memphis Area Transit Authority. The transition was complete. We had gone more than full circle, from the back of the bus to the head of the bus company. As some of the old mothers of the church would say, "Ain't God good!" Even more ironic is the fact that Will Hudson is head of the deacon board at Monumental Baptist Church where Rev. Billy Kyles is pastor. Billy Kyles is the man who was standing next to Martin Luther King when he was shot in Memphis; he was the first to kneel down and try to revive Dr. King as he lay on the balcony of the Lorraine Motel where he died.

Martin Luther King first came to national attention as the leader of the Montgomery, Alabama bus boycott after Rosa Parks refused to sit in the back of the bus. This man who knelt next to Dr. King as he died has lived to see the lay leader of his church become the president of the Memphis bus company. Yes, mothers of the church, God is indeed good!

In the months before he was killed in Memphis on April 4, 1968, Martin Luther King turned his attention to the problem of poverty in America. He had recognized that civil rights gains had not improved economic conditions for blacks. The federal government was more focused on the Vietnam War, and Dr. King wanted to refocus attention on poverty, not only black poverty but all poverty in America.

"We believe the highest patriotism demands the ending of the war and the opening of a bloodless war to final victory over racism and poverty," he said. [15] He organized the Poor People's Campaign to include a major demonstration in Washington, D.C. There was no plan for him to be in Memphis until he was asked a few weeks before his death to come and support the striking sanitation workers. His aides were divided over whether he should go to Memphis, because some were concerned it would divert energy away from planning the Washington campaign. In the end, Dr. King decided that the sanitation strike was in fact part of this larger issue of poverty in America, and he went to Memphis.

His prescription for a better America was not merely the removal of its racial barriers but the development of a society in which everyone is a genuine stakeholder. The America he lived in at that time was a country he believed had a level of economic disparity among its citizens that, if left unaddressed, would lead to a continuing conflict between the haves and the have-nots, a conflict that could ultimately destroy the entire nation. The truth, in its very simplest terms, is that the government takes our money in the form of taxes and then determines how to spend it for the common good. In theory, that is a potentially workable concept. However, in practice it has serious flaws, the most egregious being that those with the most influence on the government's decisions are people and institutions with the dangerous combination of money, greed, and vested interest. For that reason, too many decisions made by government cater to the wealthy. The obvious losers in this process are the poor. They have little influence on government, even in a democracy, unless the unrest among them demands the government's attention. In the absence of some form of open rebellion, the poor get the shaft.

---

15 Poor People's Campaign, Wikipedia.org

The Poor People's Campaign was to be that nonviolent rebellion, conceived as an organized civil disobedience campaign defined by Dr. King as "nonviolent, but militant, and as dramatic . . . as the riots without destroying property." [16] The aim of this second phase of the Civil Rights Movement was to bring together women as well as poor blacks, Chicanos, Indians, and whites. It included many in the labor movement. Together they presented an organized set of demands to Congress, an economic "bill of rights" that included a massive amount of low income housing, a commitment by government to full employment, and a guaranteed income measure.

Martin Luther King envisioned a nation in which poverty would be nonexistent: "I am now convinced," he said, "that the simplest solution to poverty is to abolish it directly by a now widely discussed measure: the guaranteed income." [17] The idea was that the government would provide a financial floor tied to the median income and not to low income. No one would fall below that floor. This idea of a guaranteed income was very much a mainstream concept in the 1970s. Daniel Moynihan, the Secretary of Labor at the time, supported it, as well as many of America's leading economists, including John Kenneth Galbraith, Paul Samuelson, and Milton Friedman.

Dr. King believed that one major source of the funding for the leveling of the economic playing field should come from a reduction in the military complex: "I refuse to accept the cynical notion that nation after nation must spiral down a militaristic

16 Ibid.

17 Bartholomew Sullivan, "King focused on ending poverty," *The Commercial Appeal*, January 18, 2010.

stairway into a hell of nuclear destruction. I believe that unarmed truth and unconditional love will have the final word in reality."[18]

Indeed, the American military complex, deployed in more than 150 countries, has its tentacles spread throughout the globe. [19] The average American has never heard of a large number of these countries and would be hard pressed to locate them on a map. The presumed purpose of our global military presence is to protect the American people. The question though is whether the nation would be more secure if its people shared its wealth so that no one lived below the poverty level. Isn't the greatest threat to our way of life the fact that vast pockets of poverty exist throughout America? There simply is not a foreign adversary capable of causing the demise of America. Any decline would come from within, because the level of poverty in America, and the confluence of wealth and power that allows it to persist, is the most dangerous enemy we face.

The issue is whether we have the resolve to truly confront and defeat poverty, since many Americans perceive an investment of resources in the economically disadvantaged as an unwarranted government handout to minorities. Although the rate of poverty among whites, at 9.4%, is much lower than the rate for blacks or Hispanics, the number of whites living in poverty is much higher. Of the 43.6 million Americans who live in poverty, about 18.5 million of them are white, and that number is increasing annually.

---

18 M.L. King Jr., Speech accepting the Nobel Peace Prize, December 11, 1964.

19 United States military deployments, Wikipedia.org

Any plan to eradicate poverty in this nation would benefit far more whites than blacks.

A shifting of resources would be at once compassionate and pragmatic. The nation can make no better investment than an investment in its own people. There has never been, and will never be, a bull market that yields a greater return on investment than this. Martin Luther King was the one person who might have moved the nation to make this happen, but it was a very controversial proposition. Some believe it is why he was killed.

I saw Dr. King in the courtyard of the Lorraine Motel just a few days before he was shot. I happened to be walking through the courtyard after having lunch at the Lorraine. I did not know him personally, and I was surprised at how easily accessible he was. He was with several of his aides. The ones I recognized were Jesse Jackson and Andrew Young. I saw no bodyguards. I could easily have walked up to him to shake his hand, because I was only a few yards away. I thought to myself that he seemed unusually unprotected given the nature of his Southern Christian Leadership Conference movement and the fact that he was in Memphis, at that time a bastion of racial mistreatment in the South.

The relative ease with which he could be accessed plays into the hands of those conspiracy theorists who have always believed that the real reason Martin Luther King was killed was not simply that he was attacking segregation in the South. These conspiracy advocates insist that he had become too influential in some highly controversial areas to remain alive. He was attacking the foundations of the enormous American military complex and the economic order of the country. They believe he was killed because his vision went much further, too much further, than merely moving from the back to the front of the bus.

CHAPTER NINETEEN

TOO MANY BLACK-EYED PEAS IN THE STEW

The Great Seal of the United States carries the simple phrase *e pluribus unum* which means "out of many, one." It has come to symbolize that out of many peoples, races, religions, and ancestries has emerged a single people and nation. In recognition of this diversity, I have often heard America referred to as a melting pot. In reality we are less like a melting pot, where each ingredient loses its individual identity, and more like a stew, where each part contributes to the whole and yet retains its own identity. In a stew, a carrot is still a carrot, a pea is still a pea, and an onion is still an onion. The challenge is to combine them in a positive way even as they retain their individual uniqueness.

In the American stew, the most difficult ingredients to combine have been blacks and whites. That flows directly from our history. To understand it, we need to go through a painful process of examining the institution of slavery. We need to ask ourselves what ever happened to those millions of slaves. Where did they go? The answer is that they are still here. They are now interspersed throughout American society. They did not go away. Too many of them evolved on their own inner city islands, the American Galapagos. [20] The need to survive without such tools as education, jobs, decent housing, and proper health care caused them to evolve into the pimps, drug pushers, prostitutes, addicts, and other such mutations as we see in the ghetto, where it can with certainty be said we have living human proof that Charles Darwin was right.

The slaves were "seasoned," the term used at the time, which meant made more suitable for use by a period of treatment in the way one might treat wood to make it more suitable for building. This seasoning of the slaves however was more sinister because it stripped away their identity to make them more suitable to serve the slave masters. A poignant sequence in the television series "Roots" is instructive.

The slave master continually cracks the whip on the African slave's back. He is demanding that the slave, Kunta Kinte, take on the new name, Toby, which the slave master had given him but which the African had refused to use. The whip cracking across his back drew tears to the slave's eyes. Then there were more lashes and more cuts across his back. Finally, with blood streaming from the cuts and tears flowing from his eyes, the slave succumbed and whispered his new name, "Toby." He was beginning to be "seasoned."

---

20 The Galapagos are islands in the Pacific Ocean where Charles Darwin ("Origin of Species") made observations that supported his theories of how species adapt through evolution in order to survive better in their environment.

But this slave was more difficult to season than some of the others. His defiance continued. He escaped and was caught several times. It was costly for a slave owner to lose his property. Finally, the slave master gave Toby a choice. He could be castrated, or he could have one foot amputated. Either way, this piece of property would escape no more. Soon Toby had a wooden foot to go with the discoloring ridges up and down his back where the whip had fallen. Only a shell remained of the once proud African. Now he was fully seasoned.

When the horrific injustices of slavery are really understood, we as a nation can begin to comprehend the underpinnings of our racial issues. To directly observe the result of evolution for many of the slaves, it is only necessary to walk around blighted inner city neighborhoods and look at the level of squalor. It is these poor that I refer to as the black-eyed peas of our society, relegated to the bottom of the American stew. For many Americans, they are faceless, but when I drive through the black ghetto, I see their individual stories. There's the one-legged beggar in the wheel chair, the prostitute waiting for the next ride, the drug runner huddled with his buyer, the gang bangers doing their thing. These descendants of the slaves have remained mired in the degradation of slavery, and they live throughout America, especially in the major cities, seven generations after slavery ended. They have become a tragic underclass that brings shame on our country.

A poor family gathers in front of this small, dilapidated house

Most Americans never see the disenfranchised. The pictures of poverty are not the pictures we see in the generic photo insert when we go to the store and buy our new wallets. Those pictures don't sell wallets. Yet they are as much a part of America as the stereotypical pictures that do sell those wallets. The niceties of America are trumpeted. Too often the face of poverty and despair is hidden in the shadows.

Residents of a neighborhood pervaded by shoddy structures
© *Dr. Ernest C. Withers, Sr. courtesy of the WITHERS FAMILY TRUST www.witherscollection.org*

The poor, the disinherited, have few advocates. There's no money in it. There will never be a lobbying firm for the disadvantaged. It is only through the will of the American people that the ultimate fate of the black-eyed peas in the American stew will be determined, and only one person in America is ever likely to be willing to serve as the lobbyist for the poor—the President of the United States.

A young man sits amidst the squalor in a back alley of the city

© Dr. Ernest C. Withers, Sr. courtesy of the WITHERS FAMILY TRUST www.witherscollection.org

The key to success of the American stew is whether the black-eyed peas become stakeholders in America. Our ultimate legacy lies in whether we have the resolve to defeat this economic and spiritual depravity in our midst. Martin Luther King had a plan to uplift these teeming masses, but he was killed just as he was beginning the effort to implement it. We have always had the ways and the means to solve this dilemma of economic injustice and its consequences for its victims and for the country. But can we ever summon the will?

CHAPTER TWENTY
A BEACON OF FAIRNESS AND JUSTICE

Sometimes I think about the young boy I once was, the boy who just wanted to eat johnnycakes and enjoy the thrill of a trip to St. Louis to see a baseball game. Whatever happened to that innocent little fellow who was simply enjoying life? I think you could just say life happened. It happens to all of us really, over many years of coming to terms with reality. If you are black in America, it happens even more so, because our reality includes challenges that are unique to the black experience. For me, life happened on the back of the bus, with the murder of Emmett Till, in being put out of the Memphis park, at a bar in New Orleans, and in countless other ways that form one's sense of the realities of life.

We all, black and white alike, must cope with disturbing events like the 9/11 terrorist attacks or the assassination of John Kennedy. When Kennedy was killed in Dallas, I remember the shock I felt and exactly where I was. When Martin Luther King was killed nearly five years later in Memphis, I remember where I was, but I was not as shocked. By that time I had come to know with certainty that the lives of very good people can come to a sudden and tragic end. When Bobby Kennedy was killed a few months later, the world had come to seem more callous, and I don't even remember where I was.

Those assassinations profoundly altered the course of American history, and we are not the same nation we would otherwise have become. Oh, if we could recapture the spirit and ideals of that era! The issues of race we have today might have been mitigated, if those who believed in a new order had lived to see their vision for America fulfilled. But the human spirit has enormous resiliency and there is a little part in all of us that is willing to believe again. The election night when Barack Obama gave his victory speech in Chicago rekindled in me a part of the passion and hope we have in our ages of innocence, but that becomes tainted as we experience life. I cried tears of joy watching television that night. I felt a sense of hope for our nation that we might now come together as One America, regardless of our particular political views.

It is hard for anyone who has not lived it to truly imagine the impact of the election of Obama on black America, especially on those who directly experienced the deep hatreds, atrocities, and exclusions in the Old South. I cried even more when I saw the old civil rights warhorse, Jesse Jackson, captured on television crying at the victory speech of the new President-elect in Chicago. What an emotional moment it must have been for Jackson, who was literally only a few feet away from Martin Luther King when he was assassinated in Memphis, to be there forty years later and only a few yards away from Barack Obama as he gave his speech. For most of us who are African-American, the slogan of that first Obama campaign, "Yes, We Can," resonated as an affirmation of our worth, just as it resonated as a vision for the future of a great nation.

From my perspective, and in many ways from an overall American perspective, no event in my lifetime has demonstrated our potential capacity to truly be one unified nation. No matter what one believes about Obama's political philosophy, it cannot be denied that this singular event spoke volumes to the world, and maybe more importantly to America itself, about how much the nation has evolved. Obama literally embodies the notion of One America. He is both black and white. He is a Christian who has an uncommon history with, and understanding of, the Muslim world.

I remembered a time in the mid-1970s when I was the administrative assistant to U.S. Representative Harold Ford on Capitol Hill. One of the other staffers, Francis, delved into transcendental meditation, and he convinced the rest of us to try it. He explained the technique, which involved the selection of your individual mantra. The mantra was simply a word or phrase that could be silently repeated to yourself during a fifteen or twenty minute period of quiet meditation. In the truest form of meditation, the mantra is taken from Hindu scripture, but of course we improvised. Francis insisted that our mantra, whatever we might choose, is an important part of the process. Indeed, continuing to silently repeat the mantra did reinforce a positive feeling and lent itself to a certain sense of calmness in the meditation process.

We could certainly use a greater measure of calmness on Capitol Hill today, but the level of rancor that exists there probably even transcends transcendental meditation. In reality, it will be everyday Americans, not the politicians, who ultimately determine who we are as a nation. It is the people who can end divisiveness. It is the people who made America the beacon of hope for mankind—not for our magnificent edifices or our military might or our economic dominance, but for our soul. It is a soul that proclaims that all are welcome to these shores and that in this land fairness and justice will ultimately prevail. And when we see that soul of America under assault by those cynics and antagonists within who would divide us, then each one of us who believes in those lofty principles on which our nation was founded should take that moment to repeat for them this simple mantra:

One America ... One America ... One America ...

EPILOGUE

I have a dream that one day on the red hills of Georgia the sons of former slaves and the sons of former slave owners will be able to sit down together at the table of brotherhood.

- Martin Luther King, Jr., March on Washington, 1963

MLK Statue on University of Texas at Austin campus © University of Texas

THANKS TO:

John and Shelley Baur
Winifred Johnson
Pam and Terry Lee
Reverend Dwight Montgomery
Madeleine Taylor
Dr. Meade Walker

SPECIAL THANKS TO:

Dorrit Gilliam
for her love and support

John T. Giberson
for his tireless effort

Jan B. King
for her consultation and advice

REFERENCES AND ACKNOWLEDGMENTS

Baldwin, J. *Nobody Knows My Name*, New York: Dial Press, 1961

chiff.com/recreation/sports/sports-stars/muhammad-ali.htm

"Census: 1 in 7 Americans lives in poverty," (Census 2010) aarp.org

Chicago Defender, September 1, 1955 per Wikipedia.org

Emmett Till, Wikipedia.org

Frazier, E. F. *Black Bourgeoisie,* New York: The Free Press, 1957

Haley, A. *The Autobiography of Malcolm X,* New York: Ballantine, 1964

Jefferson, Thomas. Autobiography, 1821 ME 1:72 per etext.virginia.edu/jefferson/quotations/jeff1290.htm

Jet, September 15, 1955 issue per Wikipedia.org

John F. Kennedy Presidential Library and Museum, Research Department, Boston, MA

malcolmx.com

Maltz, M. *Psycho-Cybernetics,* Prentice-Hall, Inc., 1960

Martin, R. G. *A Hero For Our Time,* New York: Macmillan, 1983

Memphis Publishing Company, *The Commercial Appeal* (A Scripps Howard Newspaper), various issues as noted in the text

Memphis (TN) Public Libraries & Information Center, Research Department

1968 Olympic Black Power Salute, Wikipedia.org

"Record Number of Americans Living In Poverty," (Census Bureau 2009) msnbc.msn.com

Joe Klein, "In The Arena," *Time,* December 13, 2010 issue (cover story); January 24, 2011

University of Virginia, History Department

utexas.edu/general/mlksculpture/

Warren, R. P. *Segregation,* New York: Random, 1956

The World Book Encyclopedia: Black Muslims; Brown v Board of Education of Topeka; Malcolm X; Muhammad, Elijah; Plessy v Ferguson

ABOUT THE AUTHOR

Art Gilliam is the owner-operator of WLOK Radio in Memphis, Tennessee. When he bought the radio station in 1977, he became the first African-American radio station owner in Memphis. But his radio ownership was only one example of his being a first. Art started his work in the media writing a regular weekly op-ed column for the Memphis *Commercial Appeal* newspaper as the first African-American to write for the paper. He then became the first African-American television newscaster in Memphis as weekend news anchor at WMC-TV (the NBC affiliate) in Memphis. He left Memphis to serve in the Washington congressional office of Congressman Harold Ford, Sr., the first African-American to be elected to Congress from Tennessee. While in Washington, Art was selected by the United States Jaycees as one of the Ten Outstanding Young Men in America.

Art wrote *One America* drawing on his unique experiences in America. From his life as a young black child growing up in the segregated South in the 1950s, to his educational journey to the halls of Yale University as a young teenager, to his experiences in the United States Air Force in the 1960's, and then his return to the South in the Civil Rights era, his life has given him an opportunity to experience the racial divide in the United State from many angles.

The book *One America* reflects Art's hope and vision for his country as it chronicles the changes that took place to move from a strictly segregated society to the election in 2008 of the first African-American President of the United States.

Art lives in Memphis with his wife Dorrit, where they together with their staff continue to operate WLOK Radio.

INDEX

insensitivity and white males, 127–29
interracial dating, 122–24
Isaiah, blackness and being overwhelmed by the past, 85–87

Jackie Robinson and the Brooklyn Dodgers, 23–24
Jackson, Jesse, 138, 148–49
Jeans, Samuel, 65, 66–67
Jefferson, Thomas, 7, 94, 129
Jet magazine, 39
Jewish classmates, 49–50
johnnycakes in Mama's kitchen, 14–16

Kennedy, Bobby, 54, 148
Kennedy, John F.
    assassination, 70–72, 147–48
    and civil rights movement, 54, 69–70
King, Martin Luther, Jr.
    assassination, 64, 134, 138–39, 148
    and bus boycott, 9
    Christianity and the civil rights movement, 93–94
    as hero to Negro Americans, 54, 70, 81, *151*
    "I Have a Dream" speech, 151
    and pacifism, 92
Kyles, Billy, 134

Leola "Mother" (mother)
    and Art leaving the South for prep school, 41–42, 45
    blackness and self-esteem, 107–9
    degrees and teaching career, 44
    and importance of education, 42, 44
    johnnycakes in Mama's kitchen, 14–16
    self-identification as Negro, 75–76

9/11 attacks, 71–72
1968 Olympic Games, 97–103, *104*
Norman, Peter, 97, 98–99, 103, *104*

Obama, Barack, 10, 83, 115, 148–49
Olympic Project for Human Rights, 98–99
One America, 149–50
"Over the Rainbow" lyrics, 125–26

Parks, Rosa, 9, 134
passing for white, 78–80
Plessy v. Ferguson, 34
police, white policemen in the South, 13–14, 30–31, 59
Poole, Elijah (Elijah Muhammad), 90
Poor People's Campaign, 134–36
poverty in America, 113, 134–38, 143, 144–46, *144–46*
prejudice
    and interracial dating, 122–24
    white male insensitivity and arrogance, 127–29
    white people in the North, 49–51

Quakers, 9

racism
    childhood fairgrounds visit, 17
    feelings of white superiority, 110–12
    and Head Nigger in Charge (HNIC), 80
    and murder of Emmett Till, 37–40, *40*, 41
    and white policemen in the South, 13–14
religion
    Black Muslims and Malcolm X, 89–94, *95*
    blackness and being overwhelmed by the past, 85–87

CPSIA information can be obtained at www.ICGtesting.com
Printed in the USA
LVOW10*2201270614

392133LV00001B/2/P